Employment Law for Business Students

Employment Law for Business Students

Stephen Hardy
and
Robert Upex

SAGE Publications

London ● Thousand Oaks ● New Delhi

First published 2006

SAGE Publications Ltd
1 Oliver's Yard
55 City Road
London EC1Y 1SP

SAGE Publications Inc.
2455 Teller Road
Thousand Oaks, California 91320

SAGE Publications India Pvt Ltd
B-42, Panchsheel Enclave
Post Box 4109
New Delhi 110 017

British Library Cataloguing in Publication data

A catalogue record for this book is available from
the British Library

ISBN-10 1-4129-0021-2   ISBN-13 978-1-4129-0021-8
ISBN-10 1-4129-0022-0   ISBN-13 978-1-4129-0022-5 (pbk)

Library of Congress Control Number: 2005934348

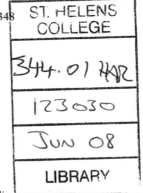
Typeset by C&M Digitals (P) Ltd., Chennai, India
Printed in Great Britain by The Cromwell Press Ltd, Trowbridge, Wiltshire
Printed on paper from sustainable resources

Contents

Illustrations and Tables

Table of Cases

Preface

A distinguishing feature of employment law is its vast interaction with business. Within a global economy, business and law exist side-by-side in the everyday flow of business transactions. Yet, in the field of employment law, business and law often collide, dealing with contractual issues, dismissal of poor-performing employees and/or business restructuring. Over the last three decades, as businesses have become more global, regulation of the workplace has simultaneously become more complex. The workplace is now highly regulated by statute and EU law, which provides new challenges to businesses, especially their HR team and/or line managers. This book arises from the need of many students of business and human resources for a book setting out the context, basic principles and key laws in relation to employment matters in business. To that end, this book provides business students with an introductory overview of employment law in a practical context.

As ever the authors both wish to warmly thank their families for their support in the writing of this book. In addition, thanks are also expressed to Mark Butler for research assistance and to our publisher, especially Kiren Shoman at Sage. The normal disclaimers apply and the law is stated as at 1 March 2006.

Stephen Hardy and Robert Upex
March 2006

1

What is Employment Law?

Employment law, or labour law as it is historically known, concerns regulation in the workplace. That is, it creates rights and responsibilities in the employment relationship, between employers and employees. It is often suggested that it relates to a cycle, an ever-revolving motion involving three tasks – creating, maintaining and terminating employment (Figure 1.1). It is ever-revolving, since as soon as a vacancy arises the cycle recommences.

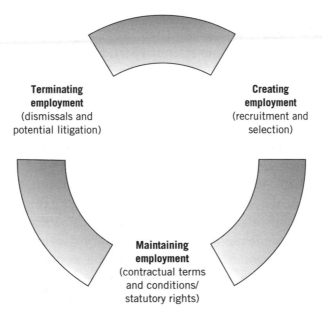

Terminating employment
(dismissals and potential litigation)

Creating employment
(recruitment and selection)

Maintaining employment
(contractual terms and conditions/ statutory rights)

Figure 1.1   The cycle of employment

DEFINING EMPLOYMENT LAW

Employment law is often labelled as either *individual*, i.e. the law relating to the employer–employee relationship, or *collective*, i.e. the relationship between the employer, the employee and a third party, normally the government and/or trade unions.

Perspective on employment law

Employment law cannot be fully appreciated unless its historical context is explained, since many of the legacies of different political ideologies and eras in both Britain and the European Union have left their mark on employment law. Below, a basic outline will chart the historical pathway of employment law.

The twelfth century to 1960 – unregulated (laissez-faire). Employment law, in its current highly regulated form, is relatively modern. It was not until the 1960s that it was deemed necessary to regulate the workplace, in terms of both safety and the employment relationship. Prior to the 1960s, *laissez-faire*, or non-interventionism, existed. The 'master–servant' relationship was the hallmark of this era, the master controlling what his servants did and did not do.

The 1960s – minimum standards and collective. In sharp contrast to the *laissez-faire* era, minimum statutory standards emerged in the 1960s. Primarily these were safety-based, but they also covered some employment rights. An example is the 1965 Redundancy Payments Act, setting out minimum payments for economic dismissal.

The 1970s – statutory. In Britain during the 1970s the 'industrial muscle' of the trade unions prevailed in a 'white hot' revolution of business change. Strikes dominated, owing to economic conditions, and management, reacting to such financial situations, brought about much change management in the workplace, causing many reorganisations, redundancies and dismissals. As a result, this era became three-dimensional (tripartite) – the trade unions and employers were involved in collective bargaining (i.e. negotiation about terms and conditions); industrial strife meant that employment relations were often hostile ('us and them'); and, whilst the government sought to readjust employment laws by removing barriers, the United Kingdom's recent membership of the then European Economic Community (now European Union) began to take effect, seeking, through the supremacy of European law over UK domestic law, to rebuild collective and minimum-standard employment rights. The latter caused conflict between a progressively developing social Europe and a Euro-sceptical British government following a US-style model.

The 1980s – individualism. A significant change of ideology came about in the 1980s, the 'Thatcher' era, as it is more commonly known. On Margaret Thatcher's rise to power in 1979 her consecutive governments sought to curb trade union power and influence. Consequently, a decline in collective bargaining between trade unions and employers occurred. The Thatcherite 'market forces' ideology sought to remove minimum standards, replacing them with freedom and individualism. During this period of employment law the employment relationship became unregulated, against EU ideals and policy. Britain in fact sought an opt-out from the European Social Charter of 1989, which set out basic employment rights for all citizens of the European Community.

The 1990s – European social compliance? The Conservative government, led by John Major, which replaced Mrs Thatcher's last administration in 1990, changed stance and sought to implement European laws, except for the Social Charter, from which Britain had negotiated an opt-out. Following such a change of position, the United Kingdom saw some basic minimum forms of regulation returning to the workplace, such as on contracts and working hours.

The twenty-first century – the 'Third Way'. Following the election of the New Labour government, under Tony Blair, in 1997 the United Kingdom signed up to the Social Charter of 1989. Further it encouraged full compliance with EU regulation in the workplace. In fact, since the mid-1990s the EU has produced a vast array of workplace regulations on working time, parental leave, part-time work, fixed-term work, business transfers and information and consultation. Consequently, the United Kingdom's new approach has been to embrace the contractual basis of modern employment law, whilst supporting it with increasing statutory minimum standards from the European Union.

Sources of employment law

The United Kingdom's sources of employment law are essentially legislation and case law. In terms of legislation, there is, at the national level, a body of both primary and secondary legislation comprising the statutory regulation of this area of law. At the EU level there are treaty provisions, directives and regulations regulating the labour law of the Member States. At the international level, there are, for example, ILO conventions which the signatory states are expected to observe. The case law from both national courts and the European Court of Justice (ECJ) is important in terms of the interpretation of this legislation. Case law is also important in that the employment relationship is based upon the contract of employment, so principles of contract derived from case law form an important part of the subject. In employment law, the main sources of law derived from cases come from the decisions of the Employment Appeal Tribunal (EAT), High Court (HC), Court of Appeal (CA) and House of Lords (HL) at domestic level, and the decisions of the ECJ and the European Court of Human Rights (ECHR) at the European level.

In addition to these two main sources of employment law there is a range of less formal 'sources', in the sense that these may have an influence on how the formal law is interpreted, applied and changed. These informal sources include: the codes of practice and reports issued by the Equal Opportunities Commission (EOC), Commission for Racial Equality (CRE), Disability Rights Commission (DRC) and the Health and Safety Executive (HSE); EU Commission recommendations; the Social Policy Agenda and the Social Dialogue at EU level. At the workplace level, informal, *voluntary* sources of law include collective and workforce agreements, works rules (i.e. the workplace rules, often contained in rule books or handbooks, issued by management to employees), and internal codes of practice and policies adopted by individual employers.

Students of employment law should be aware of these formal and informal sources of law, and of their interplay at the various levels, workplace, national, European and international.

KEY LEGISLATION

Students of employment law should have knowledge of the centrally important provisions contained in the key legislation which forms the legislative backbone of the subject. The primary legislation is the main focus of this section, although secondary legislation, mainly in the form of statutory instruments, forms an important part of regulation in this area. In the sphere of individual employment law, the Employment Rights Act (ERA) 1996 is the primary legislation dealing with, *inter alia*, the law relating to: unfair dismissal; redundancy; notice rights; protection of wages; protected disclosure; time off work; maternity, adoption and parental leave. At the collective level, the Trade Union and Labour Relations (Consolidation) Act 1992 (TULRCA) and the Employment Relations Acts 1999 and 2004 (EReLA) concerns, *inter alia*, the law governing trade unions, their relationship with their members and employers, industrial action and collective bargaining, including the important area of the statutory recognition of trade unions contained in Schedule A1 of the Act. Certain aspects of wages have been regulated by the National Minimum Wage Act 1998, which stipulates the minimum wage for certain categories of worker in any pay reference period.

Other important secondary legislation includes: the Transfer of Undertakings (Protection of Employment) Regulations 1981, SI 1981/1794 (TUPE), which safeguard certain employment rights upon the transfer of a business (or part of a business) as a going concern. These regulations were supposed to implement the Acquired Rights Directive (Directive 77/187/EC) (the ARD); the Working Time Regulations 1998, SI 1998/1833, which regulate working hours, daily and weekly rest periods and rest breaks, annual leave and night work. These regulations implement the Working Time Directive (Directive 93/104/EC, which was amended by Directive 2000/34/EC – the 'Horizontal Amending Directive': the original Directive 93/104/EC has been consolidated by Directive 2003/88/EC, in force from 2 August 2004 (the WTD); and the National Minimum Wage Regulations 1999 (SI 1999/584), which contain detailed provisions concerning the minimum wage.

In the field of discrimination law, the key statutes are the Sex Discrimination Act (SDA) 1975, the Race Relations Act (RRA) 1976 and the Disability Discrimination Act (DDA) 1995 (as amended DDA 2005), covering sex, race and disability discrimination respectively. It should be noted that these statutes regulate a wider area than employment law, as they include the provision of goods, services and facilities. Generally, the student of employment law need only concentrate on the employment parts of these statutes. The Equal Pay Act 1970 (EqPA) should be considered alongside the SDA in any study of sex discrimination law, as this statute concerns the elimination of sex discrimination from pay structures. Important (and recent) secondary legislation in the discrimination field are the Employment Equality Regulations. There are two sets of these: the Employment Equality (Religion or Belief) Regulations 2003 (SI 2003/1660) and the Employment Equality (Sexual

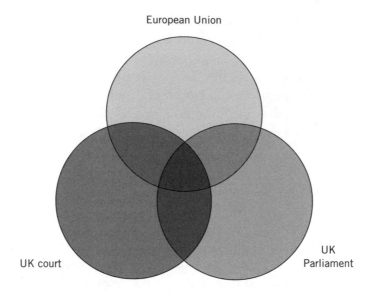

Figure 1.2   The EU influence on UK law

Orientation) Regulations 2003 (SI 2003/1661), which implement part of the Equal Treatment Framework Directive (Directive 2000/78).

Other important pieces of legislation in labour law are: the Health and Safety at Work, etc., Act (HASAWA) 1974; the Human Rights Act (HRA) 1998; and the various Employment Acts.

At EU level, Article 141 (former Article 119) of the Treaty, the provision concerning equal pay for equal work or work of equal value, has been immensely significant in the development of equal pay law at the domestic level. Furthermore, several directives have been centrally important in domestic law, e.g.:

> Equal Treatment Directive (Directive 76/207/EC) (the ETD).
> Equal Pay Directive (Directive 75/117/EC) (the EPD).
> Parental Leave Directive (Directive 96/34/EC) (the PLD).
> Part Time Workers Directive (Directive 98/2) (the PTWD).
> Acquired Rights Directive (Directive 77/187/EC) (the ARD).
> Working Time Directive (Directive 93/104/EC) (the WTD).
> Fixed-term Contracts Directive (Directive 99/70) (the FTCD).
> Equal Treatment Framework Directive (Directive 2000/78) (the ETFD).

It will be seen from the above list that EU law has had a major influence on the development of many aspects of domestic employment law.

Moreover, all of these influences (see Figure 1.2) make employment law what it is in the UK.

INSTITUTIONS

A network of key institutions exists, and students of employment law should be familiar with them.

Advisory Conciliation and Arbitration Service

ACAS was established in 1974, gaining statutory recognition under the Employment Protection Act 1975. Its head office is in London and it has eleven regional offices across the United Kingdom. It is an independent organisation, albeit that it is government-funded. It is governed by a council, consisting of a chair appointed by the Secretary of State for Trade and Industry, and nine members representing employers, trade unions and independent members (usually lawyers and/or academics).

Arbitration is a voluntary process at the collective level whereby the parties to a dispute agree to submit to the decision of an arbitrator, although the decision itself is not legally binding. (It is expected, however, that, having agreed to submit to this process, the parties will observe the terms of any decision arising from it.) Under TULRCA, s. 212, 'Where a trade dispute exists or is apprehended ACAS may, at the request of one or more of the parties to the dispute and with the consent of all the parties to the dispute,' refer the matters in dispute to arbitration. Arbitration should be considered by ACAS only after consideration has been given to whether conciliation or negotiation could resolve the dispute. (These should be attempted before arbitration is offered.) Arbitration is carried out through the Central Arbitration Committee (see below) or by an arbitrator selected from a panel of names kept by ACAS.

The 'Anti-Discussion' Commissions

There are currently three commissions in the field of discrimination law: the Equal Opportunities Commission (EOC); the Commission for Racial Equality (CRE); and the Disability Rights Commission (DRC). The EOC covers sex discrimination and equal pay, the CRE deals with race discrimination and the DRC covers disability discrimination. The government has announced that these three bodies will merge in 2007 to form a new consolidated body overseeing equal opportunities and human rights at work.

Equal Opportunities Commission

The Equal Opportunities Commission (EOC) was established under the Sex Discrimination Act 1975 (SDA), s. 53. It has a statutory duty to work towards the elimination of discrimination and to promote equal opportunities. Further, it has a duty to keep the working of the relevant legislation under review, i.e. the SDA and the Equal Pay Act 1970. The EOC can assist in bringing cases to employment tribunals and the courts. It can also undertake and/or fund research and educational activities (SDA, s. 54), as well as issue codes of practice (SDA, s. 56A). Examples are the Codes of Practice on Sex Discrimination, Equal Opportunity Policies and the Code of Practice on Equal Pay (1997). The EOC also has the power to conduct a formal investigation 'for any purpose connected with the carrying out of [its] duties' (SDA, s. 57(1)). Such formal investigations must be conducted under the provisions of the relevant regulations, the Sex Discrimination (Formal Investigations) Regulations 1975 (SI 1975/1993).

Commission for Racial Equality

The Commission for Racial Equality (CRE), which is similar to the EOC, was created by the Race Relations Act 1976. It has similar powers and duties to those of the EOC, noted above. It can issue codes of practice (RRA, s. 47). Examples include: the Code of Practice for the Elimination of Racial Discrimination (1983) and the Code of Practice on the Duty to Promote Racial Equality (2002). These codes do not have statutory force but they are admissible in evidence and may be taken into account by tribunals and courts in determining any question under the relevant statutes: see RRA, 47(10). Like the EOC, the CRE can instigate formal investigations 'for any purpose connected with the carrying out of [its] duties' (RRA, s. 48(1)), but only where they have reasonable suspicion that unlawful acts of discrimination are taking place. Formal investigations must be conducted under the provisions of the Race Relations (Formal Investigations) Regulations 1975, SI 1977/841. If, following a formal investigation, the CRE becomes satisfied that a person is committing or has committed, *inter alia*, any unlawful discriminatory acts or practices, they may issue a non-discrimination notice to employers (RRA, s. 58(2)).

Disability Rights Commission

The Disability Rights Commission (DRC) was established under the Disability Rights Commission Act 1999. From its creation on 25 April 2000 the DRC's main duties have been to work towards eliminating discrimination against disabled people; to promote equal opportunities for disabled people; to keep the DDA under review; to provide information and advice to disabled people, employers and service providers. It has the power to issue codes of practice (DDA, s. 53A) and to support individuals seeking to enforce their rights (DRCA, s. 7). It has similar powers to the other two Commissions in terms of conducting investigations and issuing non-discrimination notices, similar to the other two Commissions (DRCA, ss. 3, 4).

Commission for Human Rights and Equality

The government, following the publication of a White Paper of 12 May 2004, has indicated its intention to integrate the three relevant Commissions discussed above into a single body (see Figure 1.3). The new

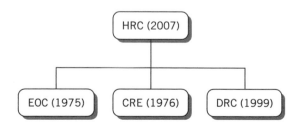

Figure 1.3   The constituents of the Human Rights Commission

unified body will have the task of promoting diversity whilst protecting equality and human rights.

Employment tribunals

Employment tribunals (ETs), formerly industrial tribunals, were established under the Industrial Training Act 1964 (see Figure 1.4) to consider employers' appeals against training levies, and their jurisdiction was extended under the Redundancy Payments Act 1965 to consider claims relating to redundancy payments. However, their jurisdictional work load has massively increased since 1972 (see Chapter 11 for further details). What is significant about employment tribunals is that they form, alongside the employment appeal tribunal (EAT), a specialist set of informal court-like institutions to adjudicate upon disputes between employers and their employees (Figure 1.4). Employment tribunals are composed of a legally qualified chair and two wing (lay) members. They are regionally organised. The EAT sits in London and Edinburgh, and is composed of a judge and two lay members.

In the next chapter we identify the employment relationship in terms of employment status.

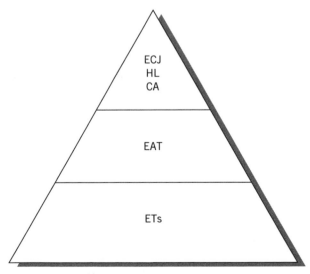

Figure 1.4   The process of employment litigation

INTERACTIVE LEARNING

1 List and explain the main sources of UK employment law.
2 What employment law institutions and how can they assist employers and employees alike in the United Kingdom?
3 Summarise the key UK legislation on employment law.

2

Employment Status

The Employment Rights Act 1996 (ERA) states that an employee is employed under a 'contract of service' or a 'contract of employment'. This relationship is to be distinguished from that of an independent contractor or self-employed person, who works under a 'contract for services'. Sometimes such persons are called 'consultants'. The distinction between the two different types of relationship lies in the nature of the obligation undertaken.

EMPLOYEES?

S. 230(1) ERA 1996 defines an 'employee' as 'an individual who has entered into or works under ... a contract of employment'. 'Contract of employment' means 'a contract of service or apprenticeship, whether express or implied, and (if it is express) whether it is oral or in writing'. There is no statutory definition of 'independent contractor' or 'contract for services'. The circular nature of this statutory definition has led the courts to lay down a series of tests in order to enable a distinction to be made between employees and self-employed, and contracts of service and contracts for services.

Multiple test

Ready Mixed Concrete (South East) Ltd v. *Minister of Pensions and National Insurance* (1968) was the first case to formulate the 'multiple' test. *Ready Mixed Concrete* concerned the question of whether the driver of a lorry was employed or self-employed, which was important in determining who was liable to pay national insurance contributions. Under the driver's contract:

1 He bought the lorry he was to drive on a hire-purchase agreement.
2 He was obliged to wear the company's colours and company insignia.
3 The lorry was similarly to be painted in the company's colours along with the company insignia.
4 Use of the lorry was for company business only.
5 The driver agreed to obey all reasonable orders 'as if he was an employee'.
6 The company could request that the vehicle be repaired, with the driver being responsible for all running and repair costs.
7 The driver was not obliged personally to drive the lorry, but was allowed to use a substitute driver.

MacKenna J found the driver to be self-employed, having considered that the driver did not necessarily contract to drive the lorry personally, as well as 'the ownership of the instrumentalities', i.e. the tools of the trade (in this case being owned by the individual and not the employer), pointed to a position of self-employment. In deciding this MacKenna J set out the conditions to be fulfilled for a contract of employment to exist. He said:

> A contract of service exists if the following three conditions are fulfilled:
>
> (i)   The servant agrees that in consideration of a wage or other remuneration he will provide his own work and skill in the performance of some service for his master.
> (ii) He agrees expressly or impliedly that in the performance of that service he will be subject to the other's control in sufficient degree to make that other master.
> (iii) The other provisions of the contract are consistent with its being a contract of service.

A more recent case in which the Court of Appeal considered this issue of who is an employee is *Express & Echo Publications Ltd* v. *Tanton* (1999). The Court of Appeal held that as a matter of law where a person is not required to perform the contract personally the relationship is not one of employee and employer.

In the later case of *MacFarlane* v. *Glasgow City Council* (2001) the EAT distinguished *Tanton's* case. The case involved qualified gymnastic instructors working at sports centres operated by the council. If an instructor could not take a class, she would arrange for a replacement from a register of coaches maintained by the council. The replacements were paid by the council, not by the applicant. Lindsay J, the then President of the EAT, said that *Tanton* was distinguishable on the grounds, among others, that the applicant could not simply choose not to work in person and that she was not free to provide any substitute, but only someone from the council's own register. Further the council paid the substitute direct. Of *Tanton* the EAT said: 'The individual there, at his own choice, need never turn up for work. He could, moreover, profit from his absence if he could find a cheaper substitute. He could choose the substitute and then in effect he would be the master.'

Mutuality of obligation test

In *O'Kelly* v. *Trusthouse Forte plc* (1983), which involved the question whether 'regular casuals', one of whom was O'Kelly, called in to work at banquets were employees. The decision of the employment tribunal was that they were not, and could not therefore complain of unfair dismissal. The determinant factor was that there was no mutuality of obligation, as they were effectively on 'standby' unless and until they were asked to come in and assist with a particular banquet. The Court of Appeal said that, as the tribunal had correctly weighed up all the factors involved in the case, there were no grounds for interfering with its decision.

The Court of Appeal did find a number of reasons that suggested that they were in fact employees, for example, that they were not in business on their own account; that the hotel had a significant amount of control over the workers; that there was a discipline and grievance procedure; and that permission was required in order to take time off from rostered duties. However, in finding that they were in fact self-employed, the Court of Appeal held that the lack of mutuality of obligation was significant. The workers had no contractual right to claim if they were not offered work, and equally, they were under no obligation to accept work which was offered.

Following its previous decisions in *Nethermere (St Neots) Ltd* v. *Taverna and Gardiner* (1984), the Court of Appeal said that a contract of employment cannot exist in the absence of mutual obligations subsisting over the entire duration of the relevant period. They said that, although the mutual obligations required to found a global contract of employment need not necessarily consist of obligations to provide and perform work, some mutuality of obligation is required. In the present case there was no mutuality of obligation: the authority was under no obligation to offer Mrs Taverna work nor was she under any obligation to accept it. She had no entitlement to any pay when she did not work and no entitlement to holiday pay or sick leave. There was thus no global contract of employment. The Court of Appeal remitted the case, however, to the employment tribunal to consider other issues, such as whether there existed a specific engagement which could amount to a contract of employment and provide the basis for an unfair dismissal claim.

The issue of casual staff was again considered by the House of Lords in *Carmichael* v. *National Power plc* (1999). The facts of the case were that the appellants worked as power station tour guides. At the time they were offered the work, they were required to sign a statement which read: 'I am pleased to accept your offer of employment as a station guide on a casual as required basis.' The guides received payment calculated by the number of hours they worked, less deductions for income tax and National Insurance payments. Owing to their position as a 'casual as required', they were not obliged to take any work, and the company did not guarantee that work would be available. The appellants claimed to be entitled to a written statement of particulars, to which they had a right only if they were employees.

The House of Lords, overruling the Court of Appeal, upheld the decision of the Employment Tribunal that the guides were not employees. Lord Irvine, who delivered the leading opinion and with whom the other Law Lords agreed, said: 'The parties incurred no obligations to accept or provide work, but at best assumed moral obligations of loyalty in a context where both recognized that the best interests of each lay in being accommodating to the other.' He said that the words 'casual as required' meant that the appellants 'were doing no more than intimate that they were ready to be invited to attend for casual work as station guides as and when the [National Power] required their services'. The 'irreducible minimum of moral obligation necessary to create a contract of service' was not present. Further, there was the fact that despite occasions where one of the two applicants was not available to accept work, disciplining that party was not an issue. Lord Irvine said that had the appeal turned exclusively on the construction of the exchange of letters he would have had no hesitation in holding as a matter of construction that there was no obligation on the company to provide work or on the guides to accept it. He said that it was clear that the parties did not intend the letters to 'constitute an exclusive memorial of their relationship' and that, in looking at the documents, the surrounding circumstances and how the parties conducted themselves, the tribunal was correct to conclude that they did not intend that their relationship should be regulated by contract.

Fiscal test

The process of deciding whether a person carries on business on his or her own account has been determined by reference to fiscal (tax) matters in *Hall* v. *Lorimer* (1992). The facts of the case were that Mr Lorimer was a skilled television technician who worked for around twenty separate companies on a series of short-term engagements. He made use of the equipment of the television company that employed him at the time. Payment was made in a lump sum plus travel expenses for each job that he undertook. Determining Mr Lorimer's employment status was important for determining the basis on which income tax was assessed.

On these facts the Employment Appeal Tribunal held that Mr Lorimer was self-employed. It stressed, however, that employment status should not be determined simply by running through some form of checklist: instead all the circumstances should be considered and evaluated accordingly: 'The whole picture has to be painted and then viewed from a distance to reach an informed and qualitative decision in the circumstances of the particular case.'

This case decides that the question whether or not there is a contract of employment is to be determined by reference to the general law of employment, as applied to all the facts of the particular case. The Court of Appeal upheld the Employment Appeal Tribunal's decision.

Conclusively, following this test, the following factors are the most important to evaluate in painting a picture of a person's work activity:

1 the contractual provisions;
2 the degree of control exercised by the 'employer';

3 the obligation of the 'employer' to provide work;
4 the obligation on the person to do the work;
5 the provision of tools, equipment, instruments and the like;
6 the arrangements made for tax, National Insurance contributions, sick pay and VAT;
7 the opportunity to work for other employers;
8 other contractual provisions, such as fees, expenses and holiday pay;
9 whether the relationship by which the person is a self-employed independent contractor is genuine or whether it is designed to avoid the employment protection legislation.

An exception

When the issue concerns health and safety rather than employment protection, particularly when a person has sustained injuries, the courts tend to treat as employees persons who might not be regarded otherwise as employees. This may be done in two ways: either by classifying the injured person as an employee, so that he or she is covered by the employer's common law duties, or by treating s. 3 of the Health and Safety at Work, etc., Act 1974 as extending the employer's obligations so as to embrace the employees of subcontractors (for example in *Lane* v. *Shire Roofing Company (Oxford) Ltd* (1995)).

In *Lane* v. *Shire Roofing* the claimant was a roofer who traded as a one-man firm, working under the category of self-employed for tax purposes. He was subsequently hired by the newly formed defendant roofing company in 1986. The defendant 'considered it prudent and advantageous to hire for individual jobs', and so hired Mr Lane on a 'payment by job' basis. While working on a particular re-roofing job the claimant fell and was injured. The central issue in the case was whether the claimant was an employee of the firm and thus owed a duty of care. In coming to this conclusion, Henry LJ, in applying the economic reality test, found that the 'business' involved in the work was that of the defendant and not the claimant. This case could have unavoidable repercussions in the health and safety context, suggesting a strict approach against finding self-employed status in this type of case. Table 2.1 summarises the current law on employment status.

Table 2.1   Employment status summarised

Employed?	Self-employed?
Pays Schedule E tax	Pays Schedule D tax
Mutuality of obligation	No mutuality of obligation
Controlled	Business on own account (own equipment/tools) – not controlled

TEMPORARY EMPLOYMENT

An interesting and expanding area in employment law is that of temporary employment. The case law in this area appears to have been developing in a way so as to fill the present lacuna in the law that leaves many 'temps' without employment rights, in particular those employed through an employment agency.

The initial position saw it as very difficult for a temporary worker to claim employment rights. Much of the difficulty arose from the need to show an 'irreducible minimum obligation' existed. In other words the employer must be obliged to offer work, whilst the worker had to be obliged to accept the work. This requirement proved difficult to overcome in earlier temporary worker cases such as *O'Kelly* v. *Trusthouse Forte plc* (1983). However, a change of attitude has been evident, with the courts suggesting it to be unjust to deny such workers employment protection merely because of their status as temporary workers. An early indication of this by the Court of Appeal can be witnessed in *McMeechan* v. *Secretary of State for Employment* (1997), where the court suggested that a temporary worker can have the status of employee in respect of each individual assignment worked. In determining this the courts must consider employment status in the context of the single engagement, rather than consider the position of the temporary worker generally. The courts have continued to develop this trend of awarding temporary workers employment rights. The Court of Appeal went even further in *Dacas* v. *Brook Street Bureau* (2004), suggesting that, in the absence of finding an express contact for service, consideration must be given to finding an implied contract.

Furthermore, a draft European Temporary Agency Workers Directive has been announced, with the principal aim of creating parity in working conditions and benefits between permanent workers and temporary workers in all twenty-five EU Member States.

A MOVABLE FEAST?

It is worth noting that the Employment Relations Act (EReLA) 1999, as amended 2004, s. 23, contains a provision which gives the Secretary of State power by order to extend employment protection rights to groups who do not enjoy them, including individuals expressly excluded from the rights. The order may confer the rights on individuals who are of a 'specified description'; it may also provide that individuals are to be treated as parties to workers' contracts or contracts of employment and make provision as to who are to be regarded as the employers of individuals. The order may also modify the operation of any rights as conferred on individuals by the order. It is not clear what steps are intended to be taken under this provision. It may be that specific groups who are currently treated as excluded from the legislation will be included within the order, for example clergy. Equally, there is no reason why the order should not be a general provision extending the relevant legislation to workers instead of employees, for example. In the latter case the effect would be considerable and would, at least to some extent, reduce the problems involved in making a distinction between employees and self-employed persons.

INTERACTIVE LEARNING

1   Decide the employment status of each of the following:

   - directors;
   - part-time workers;
   - musicians;
   - temporary workers;
   - church ministers.

2   Doris is a machinist who worked for Old Ltd for seven years in their factory. Two years ago she was offered a 'home working' contract by Old Ltd, who were anxious to reduce their overheads. Doris was keen to accept this contact because she had child care commitments, especially in the school summer holidays. Under her written home working contract Doris was informed she was now a casual worker, able to accept or reject any assignment of work offered to her by Old Ltd. Old Ltd provided her with her machine and paid an electricity allowance to cover the cost of any electricity used by Doris in her

(Continued)

(Continued)

work for them. They paid her two weeks' holiday a year and she was offered the chance to participate in a pension scheme run by Old Ltd. Doris has worked for Old Ltd throughout the last two years, apart from one week when her son was ill. During this week Old Ltd allowed her to delegate her assignment to another Old Ltd homeworker. At the time this happened she was told that if for any reason she could not accept a subsequent assignment she would not be offered a further assignment for at least four weeks. Advise Doris whether she is an employee of Old Ltd.

3 List the advantages and disadvantages of employment and self-employment.

3

Contract of Employment

The main sources of an employment contract are express terms and implied terms. Express terms are to be found in the contract itself and/or documents expressly or impliedly incorporated into the contract, such as collective agreements or employers' handbooks.

In cases where there is no employment contract, the existence of a written statement of terms and conditions under s. 1 of the Employment Rights Act (ERA) 1996 will assist the determination of what terms were agreed. An express term may in appropriate cases be qualified by an implied term, such as the term not to behave in a way such as to undermine the relationship of trust and confidence between employer and employee. Implied terms will arise where the court or tribunal regards the implication of a term as necessary to give the contract business efficacy or reflect what the parties would have agreed.

FORMING THE CONTRACT

The main source of contractual obligations is the express terms of the contract. This process is assisted by the provisions of ERA, s. 1, which requires employers to give their employees written particulars of many of the more important terms of their contracts. Terms may be expressly incorporated by a reference in the contract to another document such as a collective agreement, but not all such terms are appropriate for incorporation; other documents may also be *impliedly* incorporated.

Statutory written statements

The main statutory requirements are contained in ERA, ss. 1–7. In effect, the main terms of the contract should be set out in the written statement, covering such matters as pay, hours of work, holidays and holiday pay, sick pay, notice entitlement and the like. It is not necessary to set out details relating to pensions and pension schemes if the employee's pension rights depend upon the terms of a pension scheme set up under a provision contained in or taking effect under a statute and the provision requires the relevant body or authority to give a new employee information concerning his or her pension rights.

The statement may be given in instalments but the following particulars must all appear in a single document:

1 the names of the employer and employee;
2 the date of the start of employment with the employer;
3 the date of the start of continuous employment;
4 the details relating to pay, hours of work, holiday entitlement, the employee's job title and the employee's place of work (see ss. 1(2) and 2(4)).

The written statement must be given within eight weeks of the start of the employment.

Changing terms

The Employment Rights Act, s. 4, deals with changes in the terms and conditions covered by s. 1. Any such changes must be notified to the employee by means of a written statement within one month. It should be noted, however, that this is a procedural requirement: it does not authorise an employer to change an employee's contractual terms simply by giving notice of change. There must be a variation which is effective in law. As with the original statement under s. 1, the statement of change under s. 4 may refer to other reasonably accessible documents for the same matters as those which may be referred to by the original statement. Similarly, in the case of changes in the notice provisions to which the employee is subject, the statement of change may refer to the law or the provisions of a collective agreement which is reasonably accessible to him or her. The term 'reasonably accessible' is defined in s. 6.

The effect of written statements

Despite confusions of terminology, particularly in the case law, it is clear that a written statement given by virtue of the requirements set out in ERA, s. 1, is not itself a contract of employment. It is, of course, evidence of the contract of employment and in many cases will probably be the best evidence available. The fact, however, that it is not the contract of employment means that it is open to an employee to argue in subsequent court or tribunal proceedings that the particulars contained in the statement did not represent what was agreed between the parties. In *System Floors Ltd* v. *Daniel* (1982), approved by the Court of Appeal in *Robertson* v. *British Gas Corporation* (1983), Browne-Wilkinson J said:

> [The statutory statement] provides very strong *prima facie* evidence of what were the terms of the contract between the parties, but does not constitute a written contract between the parties. Nor are the statements of the terms finally conclusive: at most, they place a heavy burden on the employer to show that the actual terms of contract are different from those which he has set out in the statutory statement.

The earlier decision of the Court of Appeal in *Gascol Conversions Ltd* v. *Mercer* (1974) appears to suggest that a written statement is conclusive. Subsequent cases have distinguished *Gascol*, however, on the basis that in that case the employee signed the written particulars as constituting the new terms of his contract of employment, not merely the receipt for new particulars of employment. In such a case, therefore, care needs to be taken, since, if the written statement is converted into a written contract, the parties should make sure that the terms contained in it are correct. Otherwise it will not be possible for them to change it without the agreement of both parties.

The Employment Rights Act, s. 11, provides for enforcement of the employee's right to be given a written statement. That is in addition to the employee's right to sue the employer for breach of contract before the ordinary courts or, where appropriate, an employment tribunal. S. 11 enables the employee to make a reference to the tribunal for it to decide what particulars ought to have been included, in cases where either no statement has been given or the statement does not comply with what is required. Where a statement has been given but there is a dispute as to what particulars ought to have been included or referred to in it, the employer or the employee may refer the matter to the tribunal. S. 12 gives the tribunal the power to determine what particulars ought to have been included, or whether any particulars which were included should be confirmed, amended or substituted.

The Employment Act 2002 has introduced a limited penalty which may be imposed on employers who fail to give a statement under ERA, s. 1 or 4. In the case of proceedings to which EA 2002, s. 38, and Sch. 5 apply (for example, sex discrimination claims or complaints of unfair dismissal), where the tribunal finds in favour of the employee, and the employer was in breach of its duty under s. 1 or 4, the tribunal must make a minimum award of compensation in respect of the failure: see s. 38(2)–(4).

EXPRESS TERMS

The following points in relation to express terms should be noted:

1 Express terms are the principal sources of contractual obligations; starting point for a consideration of the respective rights and obligations of the parties is the contract or written statement of particulars.
2 Express terms may be written or oral or partly written and partly oral.
3 The best evidence of an express term is an express term contained in a written contract of employment, but, in the absence of such a written contract, the statutory written statement given to an employee under the Employment Rights Act 1996, s. 1, is likely to provide the best evidence, though it is not conclusive as to the terms agreed.
4 The express terms of the contract may also be found in documents expressly or impliedly incorporated into the contract, such as collective agreements or employers' handbooks.
5 If the contract contains an express term covering a particular matter such as mobility, there will be no scope for the implication of a term in relation to that matter.

6   An express term may in appropriate cases be qualified by an implied term, such as the term not to behave in a way such as to undermine the relationship of trust and confidence between employer and employee.
7   Where interpretation or construction of the contractual documentation is necessary, the court or tribunal will apply the ordinary rules of construction for contracts, including the *contra proferentem* rule.
8   An apparently wide clause, such as a flexibility clause, will not always give the employer as free a hand as its terms suggest.
9   Clauses which are apparently unreasonable may be subject to the Unfair Contract Terms Act 1977.

The Court of Appeal followed this decision in *Marley* v. *Forward Trust Group Ltd* (1986) in which the employee's contract of employment incorporated the employers' personnel manual which included the terms of a collective agreement made between the employers and the union. The agreement was expressed to be binding in honour only and included a provision that, if a redundancy situation arose, an employee who accepted redeployment would have six months in which to assess its suitability without prejudicing his right to redundancy compensation. This happened to the employee, who, after two months, informed his employers that his new position was unsuitable and that he wished to exercise his 'redundancy option'. The employers took the view that the employee had been transferred under a mobility clause in his contract and not because of a redundancy situation. They therefore treated him as having resigned. The Court of Appeal held that the terms of the collective agreement had been incorporated into the individual employee's contract (even though the agreement itself was unenforceable) and that the employers could not rely upon the mobility clause when redeploying the employee.

SPECIFIC EXPRESS TERMS

Express terms relating to the following matters are considered here:

1   mobility;
2   working time and holidays;

3 pay;
4 benefits in kind;
5 'garden leave';
6 notice (and pay in lieu of notice).

Mobility

It is advisable for an employer to include an express mobility term in the employment contract; otherwise, a term will fail to be implied. Clearly, employers who want to save argument later will be well advised to include an express clause. If a term is implied, there is the risk that the term will have a disproportionate effect which could have been avoided. In any case, ERA 1996, s. 1(4)(h), requires the written statement to specify the place of work or 'where the employee is required or permitted to work at various places, an indication of that and of the address of the employer'. The provisions of s. 1(4)(k) should also be noted. These come into operation for employees required to work outside the United Kingdom for more than one month. This should not be too difficult for an employer.

Working time and holidays

The arrangements for working time will depend upon the nature of the employer's work. For example, the employer may operate a shift system for production staff and flexitime arrangements for administrative staff; field sales staff and managers may have fixed hours. Although theoretically the employer might demand of the employee long working hours, it is possible that this might be subject to an implied restriction, arising from the decision of the Court of Appeal in *Johnstone* v. *Bloomsbury Health Authority* (1991). The effect of the Working Time Regulations 1998 (SI 1998/1833) should be noted. The regulations were introduced to implement Council Directive 93/104/EC, but not before the UK government had brought an (unsuccessful) action against the European Commission, arguing that the legal basis upon which the directive was adopted was incorrect (see *United Kingdom* v. *Commission of the European Union* (1997)).

Until the advent of the Working Time Regulations there was very limited statutory regulation of holiday rights and in practice an employee's entitlement to holiday depended upon the terms of the employment contract. Now regulations 13 and 16 entitle workers to four weeks' annual paid leave in each leave year (as defined by regulation 13(2)). There are detailed provisions dealing with the dates on which leave may be taken, which entail either party giving notice within prescribed time limits and containing prescribed information. An employer wishing to escape these provisions may do so by having a 'relevant agreement', in practice a collective agreement or employment contract: see the definition in regulation 2(1). Leave may not be bought out unless the worker's employment is terminated (see reg. 13(9)).

'Garden leave' clauses

A 'garden leave' clause is a clause found in employment contracts by which the employer reserves the right to require the employee not to perform his or her duties as an employee but agrees that he or she will continue to be paid. Such clauses have so far given rise to relatively little case law and such case law as there is has tended to be concerned with the principles upon which injunctions are granted.

An important case to consider as regards the 'garden leave' clause is *Provident Financial Group plc* v. *Hayward* (1989). The employee's contract as financial director provided that, during the continuance of his employment, he would not 'undertake any other business or profession or be or become an employee or agent of any other person or persons or assist or have any financial interest in any other business or profession.' Another clause provided that the company was under no obligation to provide him with work but could suspend from performance of his duties or exclude him from any premises of the company, but his salary was not to cease to be payable by reason only of the suspension or exclusion.

Despite case law recognising the validity of garden leave clauses, uncertainties do remain, since an excessively long period of notice linked with garden leave might be held to be in restraint of trade and thus void and unenforceable.

It is unlikely that in the absence of an express garden leave provision the court would be prepared to imply such a provision.

Notice

At common law the parties are free to choose whatever notice provision they like, though an employer who sought to impose an excessively long period of notice on an employee might be prevented from doing so by the doctrine of restraint of trade. If the contract of employment does not specify a notice period a reasonable period of notice will be implied. In most cases where there are no express notice provisions the situation is likely to be governed by ERA, s. 86, which gives a statutory right to a minimum period of notice. Employees continuously employed for one month or more but less than two years are entitled to at least one week's notice. After two years' employment, employees are entitled to one week's notice for each year of continuous employment, but, if they have been employed for more than twelve years, their statutory entitlement will not exceed twelve weeks. S. 86(2) obliges an employee continuously employed for one month or more to give at least one week's notice. The notice must be definite and explicit and must specify the date of termination or give sufficient facts from which the date of termination can be ascertained (*Morton Sundour Fabrics Ltd* v. *Shaw* (1967) and *Walker* v. *Cotswold Chine Home School* (1977)). Once a notice has been given, it cannot be withdrawn unilaterally, but only with the agreement of the other party (*Riordan* v. *War Office* (1959) 3 and *Harris and Russell Ltd* v. *Slingsby* (1973)). Although an attempt to provide for a shorter period will be ineffective, s. 86(3) provides that either side may waive his or her right to notice or accept a payment in lieu of notice.

IMPLIED TERMS

The following points should be noted:

1   Even if the employer complies with the requirements of ERA, s. 1, and gives a written statement or decides to give an employee a full written contract of employment, there are likely to be areas in the

contract which are not covered by express terms and where the court or tribunal will have to consider resorting to implied terms to fill the apparent gap.

2   A term will be implied only where there is no express term governing the matter in dispute.

3   If a term is implied the term will be no broader than is necessary to give efficacy to the contract.

4   An express term may in some cases be qualified by an implied term.

5   There is a difference between terms such as mobility/flexibility, terms which have to be determined according to the particular contract, and 'status' or 'legal incidents' terms which, where used, establish rules for contracts of employment as a class.

At common law a breach by either party of an implied term may give the other party the right to terminate the contract without notice. Thus a breach of an implied term by the employer may give the employee the right to resign and argue that the breach was so significant as to amount to a repudiation and to entitle him or her to treat the contract as at an end. In the context of the statutory right not to be unfairly dismissed this is usually called constructive dismissal. In other contexts it is probably best called wrongful repudiation or simply a breach of contract.

The implication of terms was considered by the House of Lords in *Liverpool City Council* v. *Irwin* (1977), in which Lord Wilberforce said:

> Where there is, on the face of it, a complete bilateral contract, the courts are sometimes willing to add terms to it, as implied terms: this is very common in mercantile contracts where there is an established usage: in that case the courts are spelling out what both parties know and would, if asked, unhesitatingly agree to be part of the bargain. In other cases, where there is an apparently complete bargain, the courts are willing to add a term on the ground that without it the contract will not work – this is the case, if not of *The Moorcock* … itself on its facts, at least of the doctrine of *The Moorcock* as usually applied. This is … a strict test.

It is important to note that both parties to the employment relationship have well established implied terms with which they must comply.

The employees have the following terms implied into their employment contract:

1   The duty to obey lawful and reasonable instructions given by the employer.
2   That the employee is reasonably competent to do the job.
3   The employee impliedly agrees to take reasonable care in the performance of his or her duties under the contract.
4   The duty of loyalty and fidelity.
5   The duty not to disclose confidential information.
6   The implied term of mutual trust and confidence.

As for the employer, the implied terms include:

1   The duty to pay wages. (It must be noted that generally this does not extend to the providing of work.)
2   A duty of care in respect of an employee's health and safety.
3   A duty to take care when producing an employee's reference.
4   The implied term of mutual trust and confidence.

EMPLOYEES' OBLIGATIONS

An employee is under an obligation to obey lawful and reasonable instructions given by the employer. This is a fairly wide obligation, which in effect enshrines the employer's managerial prerogative. It extends beyond the normal situation of obedience to instructions given in the workplace to such issues as mobility and the need to adapt to changes in working practice, as in *Cresswell* v. *Board of Inland Revenue* (1984). There the employees tried to argue that the Inland Revenue was in breach of their terms of service in requiring them to operate the proposed computerisation of the PAYE system. Walton J held that, although the proposed introduction of computerisation changed the way the employees performed their duties, they were still administering the PAYE system and performing the duties of tax officers. He said, however, that this was subject to the proviso that the employer must provide any necessary training or retraining for them. If, however, the nature of the work alters so radically that it is outside their contractual obligations, it will not be reasonable to expect employees to adapt.

It is an implied term in a contract of employment that the employee is reasonably competent to do the job. Thus a serious act of incompetence may justify the employer in terminating the contract summarily at common law.

Similarly, the employee impliedly agrees to take reasonable care in the performance of his or her duties under the contract. Although the employer will usually be vicariously liable for the employee's act of negligence, theoretically the employer may sue the employee for an indemnity for breach of the duty of care, as in *Lister* v. *Romford Ice & Cold Storage Co. Ltd* (1957). In appropriate circumstances, carelessness may justify summary dismissal at common law, though clearly it would have to satisfy the general principle that it was so serious as to amount to a repudiation on the employee's part of his or her contractual obligations: (see *Power* v. *British India Steam Navigation Co. Ltd* (1930) and *Jupiter General Insurance Co. Ltd* v. *Shroff* (1937)). In this last case, an act of negligence by a manager was held to amount to serious misconduct justifying summary dismissal. So too in *Baster* v. *London and Country Printing Works* [1899] a single act of forgetfulness by an employee which caused damage to a valuable machine used in the employer's printing business was held to justify summary dismissal.

The following points should be noted:

1   An employer may rely upon the implied duty of loyalty and fidelity as an alternative to an express restrictive covenant or in the absence of such a covenant.
2   The implied term may be used against an employee during the currency of the employment or after it has ended.
3   Enforcement is likely to be means of an injunction.

It is well established that there is a duty lying on the employee not to disclose confidential information, but the courts have had difficulty in establishing what amounts to confidential information in any particular case. A distinction must be made between an individual employee's general knowledge or individual skill, which he or she may legitimately put to use in the future, and a trade secret which the employer is entitled to protect. In *Printers and Finishers Ltd* v. *Holloway* (1964), Cross J said:

> The mere fact that the confidential information is not embodied in a document but is carried away by the employee in his head is not of itself a reason against the granting of an injunction to prevent its use or disclosure by him. If the information in question can fairly be regarded as a separate part of the

employee's stock of knowledge which a man of ordinary honesty and intelligence would recognise to be the property of his old employer and not his own to do as he likes with, then the court, if it thinks that there is a danger of the information being used to the detriment of the old employer, will do what it can to prevent that result by granting an injunction. Thus an ex-employee will be restrained from using or disclosing a chemical formula or a list of customers which he has committed to memory.

EMPLOYER'S OBLIGATIONS

The general rule at common law is that an employer is not obliged to provide work for the employee to do but only to pay the wages due under the contract. The classic statement of this rule is that of Asquith J in *Collier* v. *Sunday Referee Publishing Co. Ltd* (1940):

> It is true that a contract of employment does not necessarily, or perhaps normally, oblige the master to provide the servant with work. Provided I pay my cook her wages, she cannot complain if I choose to take any or all of my meals out.

There are, however, exceptions to the general rule which have arisen in cases where the law has recognised that in certain types of contract it is essential to the contract that the employee is given the opportunity to work. So, for example, it will be a breach of contract to fail to provide work for an employee paid on a piecework or commission basis, as in *Devonald* v. *Rosser & Sons* (1906) and *Turner* v. *Goldsmith* (1891). In this last case, the Court of Appeal said that an agent paid on a commission basis was entitled to be sent a reasonable amount of work to enable him to earn his commission. See also *Bauman* v. *Hulton Press Ltd* (1952).

Another group of exceptions arises in cases where the nature of the work is such that the opportunity for publicity is as important as the remuneration paid to the employee. This applies to actors, singers and the like. Thus, for example, in *Marbé* v. *George Edwardes (Daly's Theatre) Ltd* (1928), a well known actress was engaged by the managers of a theatre to play a particular part in a play. There was also a collateral agreement by which the managers undertook to advertise her name in a prominent position. On the day of the dress rehearsal they refused to allow her to appear in the part. The Court of Appeal held that the contract imposed an express obligation upon the managers to allow her to appear in the part as agreed. They also held that damages for breach of that obligation might include compensation for loss of reputation. A similar decision was reached by the House of Lords in *Clayton and Waller Ltd* v. *Oliver* (1930), which expressly approved *Marbé's* case.

These cases concern the loss of opportunity for an actor or actress to enhance his or her reputation and arise in circumstances where the contract specifically contemplated such an enhancement of reputation. They show also that the obligation may be to provide work of a particular kind or standard (for example, a particular role or part), rather than any work.

The obligation lying upon the employer to pay the employee the wages which are due is at the heart of the employment contract. Normally, the contract will contain express provisions dealing with the remuneration due, and it is a statutory requirement that details of the scale, rate or method of calculation of the remuneration should be given to the employee in writing: see ERA, s. 1(4)(a) and (b). Employees also have a statutory right, under ERA, s. 8, to receive an itemised pay statement upon payment of wages or salary.

In the event of there being no express term governing pay, the court or tribunal would imply a term, no doubt to the effect that the employee should receive 'the going rate for the job'. Alternatively, the employee would be able to recover on the basis of *quantum meruit*, as in *Way* v. *Latilla* (1937), where there was an understanding that the employer would look after the employee's interests.

The employment relationship between employer and employee includes the important common law duty to care for the employee's health and safety and the duty to take care in the compilation of references for the employee.

The decision of the House of Lords in *Wilsons & Clyde Coal Co. Ltd* v. *English* (1938) establishes that the employer owes a duty to an employee to provide competent and safe fellow employees, to provide adequate materials and to provide a safe system of working. It may be a corollary of the first aspect of this duty that an employer is under a duty to take steps to terminate the employment of a potentially dangerous employee.

Although the duty is generally regarded as arising in the law of tort, it gives rise to a contractual obligation on the part of the employer to act reasonably in matters of safety. This means that an employee who resigns because of the employer's failure in this respect may claim to have been constructively dismissed. So, for example, in *British Aircraft Corporation Ltd* v. *Austin* (1978) the employer's failure to investigate the employee's complaint about the protective eyewear provided was held by the EAT to amount to conduct entitling him to resign without notice. In such a case, however, the breach by the employer must be sufficiently serious as to amount to a repudiation of the contract.

There are suggestions in *Johnstone* v. *Bloomsbury Health Authority* (1991) that the express terms in an employee's contract may be qualified by the implied duty of care owed by the employer. In the case in question, the employee's contract stipulated that his hours of duty should consist of a standard forty-hour week and an additional availability on call up to an average of forty-eight hours a week over a specified period. A majority of the Court of Appeal said that the employers were not entitled to require the employee to work so many hours in excess of his standard working week as would foreseeably injure his health. Stuart-Smith LJ suggested that the employers' power under this contractual provision had to be exercised in the light of their implied duty of care, but Sir Nicolas Browne-Wilkinson V-C merely said that they had the right, subject to their ordinary duty not to injure the employee, to call upon him to work those hours up to the stipulated maximum.

Even where an express term is being considered, constraints of this term may be implied where it is reasonable to do so. The case of *United Bank* v. *Akhtar* (1989) suggests that an express term may indeed be qualified by an implied term. In this case United Bank wished to transfer Mr Akhtar to an alternative branch. In his contract of employment a mobility clause in extremely broad terms was expressly included. However, Mr Akhtar, owing to certain personal circumstances, requested that the transfer be postponed, a request which was dismissed. As a result Mr Akhtar applied for twenty-four days' paid leave in order to put his personal affairs in order, a request which received no response. Mr Akhtar's pay was subsequently stopped, resulting in a claim of constructive dismissal.

In considering the construction and nature of the express mobility clause the Employment Appeal Tribunal implied a term to control the discretion the employer had with regards such an express term. In other words, despite the wide-ranging effects the mobility clause was expressed to include, the employer could only utilise their contractual right to the point of reasonableness.

MUTUAL TRUST AND CONFIDENCE

In *Wilson* v. *Racher* (1974) Edmund-Davies LJ observed that 'a contract of service imposes upon the parties a duty of mutual respect'. This case was decided when the law relating to unfair dismissal was in its infancy. Since the decision of the Court of Appeal in *Western Excavating (ECC) Ltd* v. *Sharp* (1978), however, which emphasised that constructive dismissal will take place only where the employer is in breach of an express or implied term in the contract and the breach is so serious as to amount to repudiation of the contract, this implied duty has been considerably refined and developed, particularly as far as the employer's behaviour is concerned. Subsequent case law has shown that the duty is flexible and will tend to vary with the circumstances of any particular case.

The scope of the term was examined by Lord Steyn in *Mahmud* v. *Bank of Credit and Commerce International SA* (1997). He approved the formulation of the term as set out by Browne-Wilkinson J above. Subsequently the Court of Appeal made it clear that tribunals should follow that formulation and not use language which might detract from the correct test or suggest that a different test has been applied: see *Transco plc* v. *O'Brien* (2002). In this last case the Court of Appeal held that the employer had been in breach of the implied term in failing to offer an employee a new contract when offering one to all other permanent employees, despite the employer's mistaken belief (arrived at in good faith) that he was not a permanent employee. As Hart J observed in *University of Nottingham* v. *Eyett* (1999), the terms in which the duty have been expressed have been 'in the negative form of prohibiting conduct calculated or likely to produce destructive or damaging consequences, rather than as positively enjoining conduct which will avoid such consequences'.

Once such a breach of the implied term has been established, the next question concerns the extent of the damages that is available. The case law has left this area rather uncertain and confused, at times being considered not to include non-pecuniary losses (see *Addis* v. *Gramaphone* (1909)), and at other times to compensate for non-pecuniary 'stigma' damages, such as damage to reputation (see *Malik* v. *BCCI* (1998)). Two House of Lords cases sought to clarify this issue: *Johnson* v. *Unisys Ltd* (2001) and *Dunnachie* v. *Kingston upon Hull City Council* (2004). These two cases appear to put a halt to the trend witnessed in the *Malik* case towards allowing compensation for damages of a non-economic nature, and returned to the traditional position of *Addis*.

In *Johnson* v. *Unisys* (2001) Mr Johnson, following a successful unfair dismissal claim against Unisys in 1994, commenced an action in the county court for damages, claiming that there had been various breaches of the implied terms of his employment contract, including the implied term of mutual trust and confidence. These breaches were alleged to have arisen owing to the lack of a hearing prior to his dismissal, and also because the company did not follow its own disciplinary procedure. Mr Johnson alleged that the manner and fact of his dismissal caused him to suffer a mental breakdown, and also made it impossible for him to find subsequent work.

On appeal to the House of Lords, Mr Johnson's claim was dismissed. The House of Lords affirmed the principle, as previously held in *Addis* v. *Gramophone*, that the scope and extent of damages were not such as to include any distress caused by the unfair manner of the dismissal or any harm caused to the employee's reputation. Their lordships also dismissed the idea that a claim for breach of mutual trust and confidence could be constructed by merely recycling the same facts used for a wrongful dismissal claim.

In *Dunnachie* (2004) there was further examination as to whether a breach of the implied term of mutual trust and confidence would extend to include compensation for non-economic loss. This issue was answered in the affirmative before an employment tribunal. The tribunal interpreted s. 123 of the Employment Rights Act 1996 (that the compensatory award for unfair dismissal was to be 'such amount as the tribunal considers just and equitable in all the circumstances' having regard to the 'loss' sustained by the complainant in consequence of the dismissal in so far as that loss was attributable to action taken by the employer) as including a sum for injury to feelings.

The House of Lords, allowing the appeal, held that 'loss' in s. 123(1) of the Act did not allow the recovery of anything other than economic loss. First, their lordships considered the origin of the provision in question, which goes back to s. 116(1) of the Industrial Relations Act 1971. It was held that s. 116(1) excluded non-economic loss and that nothing in the re-enactment suggested that this position had altered. Furthermore, their lordships read the phrase 'just and equitable' as a tool of flexibility available for the tribunal to utilise when making an appropriate award, rather than defining the scope of the 'loss'.

INTERACTIVE LEARNING

1   List the express and implied terms, giving examples for each.
2   'The obligation to maintain mutual trust and confidence ensures fair dealing between the employer and employee in respect of disciplinary proceedings, suspension of an employee and dismissal.' Consider this statement, using case law to illustrate your answer.

4

Equal Pay

In modern business equal pay legislation is necessary to eliminate sex discrimination from pay systems, and therefore to close the so-called 'gender pay gap', i.e. the difference in pay between men and women who do equal work. Equal pay is governed by the 1970 Equal Pay Act (EqPA), as amended by European law. Thus the overriding principle that men and women should receive equal pay for the same work or work of equal value is enshrined in Article 141 of the EC Treaty. The Equal Pay Directive (Directive 75/117/EEC) ('EPD') provides more detailed provisions relating to pay and concerns the application of Article 141, and the Equal Treatment Directive (Directive 76/207/EEC) ('ETD') may also be relevant in interpreting equal pay law.

PAY

Article 1 of the Equal Pay Directive provides that the principle of equal pay 'means, for the same work or for work to which equal value is attributed, the elimination of all discrimination on grounds of sex with regard to all aspects and conditions of remuneration'. The EOC, using powers given by SDA, s. 56A, has issued a Code of Practice on Equal Pay ('the Code') whose objective is 'to provide practical guidance and recommend good practice to those with responsibility for or interest in the pay arrangements within a particular organisation'. The Code is admissible in evidence in proceedings under the EqPA (SDA, s. 56A).

What is equal pay?

The EqPA covers all *contractual* benefits, whereas Article 141 applies to 'remuneration' an employee receives from her employer, including contractual benefits, gratuitous benefits and any benefits which the employer is required to provide by statute. However, 'pay' has been given a very wide meaning and been held by the ECJ to include, for example: concessionary, non-contractual travel facilities (*Garland* v. *British Rail Engineering Ltd* (1982)); statutory redundancy payments (*Barber* v. *Guardian Royal Exchange Assurance Group* (1990)) and benefits paid under private, occupational pension schemes (*Barber* v. *Guardian Royal Exchange Assurance Group* (1990)). This is because it arises 'by reason of the existence of the employment relationship'.

The Equal Pay Act 1970, which came into force at the same time as the SDA in 1975, is the domestic statute dealing with equal pay between men and women. The EqPA seeks to eliminate gender-based pay discrimination, so that differences in pay between men and women are allowed, provided they are due to factors other than sex, e.g. performance-related pay, pay to reward qualifications achieved, or, arguably, pay based on seniority. (See the discussion of the genuine material factor defence below.) Therefore it is a defence for the employer to show that the pay disparity is due to factors other than sex.

BRINGING AN EQUAL PAY CLAIM

To bring a successful equal pay claim, the woman must establish that she is in the same employment (or working for an associated employer) as the selected comparator(s) of the opposite sex, who is/are engaged on one of the following three situations:

1 like work;
2 work rated as equivalent, i.e. work which has been given an equivalent rating under a job evaluation study (JES); or
3 work which is of equal value (EqPA, s. 1(2)(a), (b), (c): these requirements are discussed below).

The equality clause operates where any term of the woman's contract is or becomes less favourable; it modifies the woman's contract of employment by raising the less favourable term in her contract so that it is not less favourable when compared with that of her male comparator.

Unlike the SDA, where a hypothetical person may be selected, the claimant must choose an actual comparator (although more than one is permissible) of the opposite sex who is engaged on like work, work rated as equivalent or work of equal value (EqPA, s. 1(2)). The choice of comparator is left to the claimant, but selecting the wrong (i.e. inappropriate) comparator will prove fatal to the claim (see *Ainsworth* v. *Glass Tubes and Components Ltd* (1977): the EAT held that an employment tribunal could not substitute for the applicant's choice of comparator another man whom it thought more appropriate).

The EqPA requires the claimant and her comparator to be in the 'same employment' (EqPA, s. 1(2) and (6)). Under s. 1(6), they are in the same employment if the comparator is employed by the same employer or an associated employer and either (1) the comparator is employed at the same establishment as the claimant or (2) he is employed at a different establishment of the employer (or an associated employer) but common terms and conditions of employment apply to both establishments.

In *British Coal Corporation* v. *Smith* (1996), HL, over 1,200 female canteen workers and cleaners working in a number of different establishments chose as their equal value comparators 150 male workers who were either surface mineworkers or in clerical posts. Their terms and conditions were governed by a national agreement, although there were some local variations, i.e. their terms and conditions were not exactly the same. The House of Lords held the terms of the comparators did not need to be identical to the claimants'; they had only to be 'on a broad basis, substantially comparable'. In this case, the comparators were held to be in the same employment, as in *Leverton* v. *Clwyd County Council* (1989), HL.

The ECJ gave the same ruling in *Allonby* v. *Accrington and Rossendale College* (2004) where the applicant college lecturer who had been dismissed rejoined the college via an agency which placed her with the college. She was carrying out the same work (on lower pay) on a self-employed basis, and used as her comparator a male lecturer at the college. The ECJ ruled that such a comparison failed under Article 141, since pay could not be attributed to a 'single source': the college and the agency were separate sources.

LIKE WORK

One of the situations in which a woman may bring an equal pay claim is where she is engaged on like work with her comparator. S. 1(4) defines 'like work' as work that is 'of the same or a broadly similar nature, and the differences (if any) between the things she does and the things they do are not of practical importance in relation to terms and conditions of employment'. When comparing the two jobs, 'regard shall be had to the frequency or otherwise with which any such differences occur in practice as well as to the nature and extent of the differences.'

The question is whether the differences (if any) between the two jobs are of practical importance. If the employer claims a difference between the jobs, it is for the employer to establish that the difference is of practical importance in relation to the terms and conditions. For example, in *Shields* v. *E. Coomes (Holdings) Ltd* (1978) the employer claimed that male counter staff at its betting shop were paid a higher hourly pay than female counter workers because of the risk of robbery, and the men were employed for security reasons. In fact the men had never been called upon to perform any security function, and the Court of Appeal held that, as the men had never been required to deal with any disturbance or attempted violence, the jobs were essentially the same. However, a difference in the responsibilities between the woman and her comparator may be a difference of practical importance, as in *Eaton Ltd* v. *Nuttall* (1977), where an error by a female scheduler who dealt with items worth about £2.50 each would have been less significant than those of a male scheduler (the comparator) who dealt with items worth between £5 and £1,000. The time the work that is carried out is not necessarily a difference of practical importance (*Dugdale* v. *Kraft Foods* (1977)), although the ECJ has held that a difference in qualifications, training and experience between the claimant and the comparator was a significant difference justifying a difference in pay (*Angestelltenbetriebsrat der Wiener Gebietskrankenkasse* v. *Wiener Gebietskrankenkasse* (1999), ECJ).

Where work has been rated as equivalent under a job evaluation study (JES) under which the claimant's and the comparator's job have been rated as equivalent, an equality clause may be inserted, under s. 1(2). Claims under this provision depend upon the employer having carried out a JES, which is probably why so few claims are brought under this part of the EqPA.

S. 1(5) requires that the jobs of the comparator and the applicant have been given equal value 'in terms of the demand made on a worker under various headings (for instance effort, skill, decision)', or where they would have been given equal values but for the JES itself being discriminatory. There are a number of methods of job evaluation, although only the 'points assessment' and 'factor comparison' systems satisfy the requirements of s. 1(5), since the JES must be analytical and objective.

Genuine material factor defence

If a claimant establishes that she is paid less than her male comparator who is engaged on like work, work rated as equivalent, or work of equal value, the employer may raise the defence that the difference in pay is not due to sex discrimination, and is a material difference between the claimant's case and the comparator's. This is the genuine material factor defence (GMF) under s. 1(3). If the employer succeeds in this defence, the equality clause will not be implied to modify the claimant's contract. Where the complaint is based on like work or work rated as equivalent, the defence *must* be a material difference between the woman's case and the man's; where it is an equal value claim, it may be a material difference.

In the GMF defence, the employer must identify a factor which is (1) the genuine cause of the difference in pay; (2) is material; and (3) is not the difference if sex. The requirement of genuineness means that the reason put forward by the employer must not be a sham or a pretence (*Strathclyde Regional Council* v. *Wallace* (1998), HL). In *Wallace*, their lordships held that a material factor must be 'significant and causally relevant'. The employers argued that the pay disparities came about through different promotion structures of teachers and financial constraints. The House of Lords held that an employer is not required to justify its pay system in every case where unequal pay is alleged. The need to establish objective justification arises only where the factor relied upon is indirectly discriminatory.

It is not possible to provide an exhaustive list of factors which may satisfy the GMF defence requirements. Case law establishes that a number of grounds have been upheld. For example, the 'market forces' defence may succeed: in *Rainey* v. *Greater Glasgow Health Board* (1987) the House of Lords held that the pay difference between employees in the NHS prosthetic fitting service, which was facing staff shortages, and those recruited from the private sector had been objectively justified, since market forces meant that in order to recruit from the private sector commercial rates of pay had to be offered. This case concerned Mrs Rainey, who worked as a prosthetist in the National Health Service. Owing to recruitment shortages, the Health Board needed to attract extra prosthetists into the service. Recruitment of practitioners from the private sector was pursued, but on their existing salaries, not on NHS rates. In effect, this policy created a pay difference between Mrs Rainey and her male comparator of £2,790 p.a.

The House of Lords held that the difference in pay was justified, because there was an objective justification for putting the man into a higher scale on entry, given the difficulty in recruitment. Lord Keith said:

> The difference must be 'material', which I would construe as meaning 'significant and relevant', and it must be between 'her case and his'. Consideration of a person's case must necessarily involve consideration of all the circumstances of that case. These may well go beyond which is not happily described as 'the personal equation', that is, the personal qualities by way of skill, experience or training which the individual brings to the job. Some circumstances may on examination prove to be not significant or not relevant, but others may do so, though not relating to the personal qualities of the employer. In particular, where there is no question of intentional sex discrimination, whether direct or indirect (and there is none here), a difference which is connected with economic factors affecting the efficient carrying on of the employer's business or other activity may well be relevant.

The House of Lords adopted the proportionality test as formulated in *Bilka-Kaufhaus GmbH* v. *Karn Weber von Hartz* (1986). In essence, the ECJ in *Bilka*, when interpreting Article 141, laid down the burden on the employer to show that the condition applied, which is having a disparate effect on one group, can be 'objectively justified'. In order to satisfy this requirement, a tripartite test was laid down, requiring the employer to show that the condition in question did 'correspond to a real need on the part of the undertaking, and are appropriate with a view to achieving the objectives pursued and are necessary to that end'.

REMEDIES

All equal pay claims must be brought in the employment tribunal (EqPA, 2(1)), and the claimant may rely upon EC law in the tribunal as well as the domestic legislation. It is not only an employee who may make an application under the EqPA: under s. 2(1A) employers may apply to the ET for a declaration where there is a dispute over the effect of an equality clause. The Secretary of State may also bring proceedings where it appears that the employer of any women is or has been in breach of a term modified or included by an equality clause and it is not reasonable to expect the women themselves to bring proceedings (e.g. because they do not have a union to support their claim): s. 2(2). The EOC is also empowered to seek a ruling from a tribunal as to whether an employer has infringed a term modified or included by an equality clause, to enable it to exercise its powers under SDA, ss. 71 and 72, to apply for an injunction to restrain persistent discrimination (s. 73, SDA).

Equal pay claims must be brought within six months of leaving the employment to which the claim relates (s. 2(4)). This time limit was challenged in *Preston and others* v. *Wolverhampton Healthcare NHS Trust* (2000), ECJ, as being incompatible with EC law. The claimants were part-time teachers employed on fixed-term contracts who argued that the six months' limit applied to the entire employment relationship, rather than the particular fixed-term contracts. The ECJ held that the six months' rule was not incompatible with EC law, provided that the limitation period was no less favourable for actions based on Community law than for actions based on domestic law. See also *National Power plc* v. *Young* (2001), CA, where the Court of Appeal held that the word 'employment' in s. 2(4) does not refer to the particular job on which the woman bases her claim but rather to the contract of employment.

INTERACTIVE LEARNING

1   What were Europe's goals when enacting the Equal Pay Directive in 1975?
2   Devise a strategy for managing equal pay. List the common pitfalls.
3   What amendments were made to the Equal Pay Act 1970 by the Employment Act 2002?

5

Discrimination

Under English law, discrimination law covers:

1 gender (including sexual orientation and a change of sex, i.e. transsexuality);
2 race;
3 disability;
4 religion or belief.

Discrimination against transsexuals was initially rendered unlawful through a ruling of the European Court of Justice (ECJ) in the case of *P. v. S. and Cornwall County Council* (1996), but was put on a statutory footing from 1 May 1999 by the Sex Discrimination (Gender Reassignment) Regulations 1999 (SI 1999/1102), which amended the Sex Discrimination Act. Discrimination on the ground of sexual orientation and religion or belief was made unlawful in December 2003 by regulations implementing provisions of the Equal Treatment Framework Directive 2000 (Directive 2000/78/EC (ETFD). These grounds of discrimination are discussed below.

There is no legislation making age discrimination unlawful, but the ETFD requires Member States to introduce such legislation by 2006. Therefore, it is likely that the United Kingdom will introduce such legislation by October 2006.

GENDER AND RACE DISCRIMINATION

There are distinct types of discrimination under both the Sex Discrimination Act and the Race Relations Act, with similar definitions:

1   direct discrimination;
2   indirect discrimination;
3   harassment;
4   victimisation.

It is important to stress the fact that direct discrimination cannot be justified under the SDA or the RRA, whereas indirect discrimination may be.

Marital status

The SDA makes unlawful discrimination against married persons in
respect of employment (SDA, s. 3(1)). A case on this issue is *Chief
Constable of Bedfordshire Constabulary* v. *Graham* (2002), EAT. Mrs
Graham was an inspector in the Bedfordshire Police. She later married a
superintendent in the same force. When an inspector post became available in the same division as her husband's, Mrs Graham made an application and was duly appointed. However, the Chief Constable was
concerned about the appointment because it would place her in a difficult position should she be required as a witness against her husband in
criminal proceedings, and it might have caused difficulty for officers
under her supervision to bring a complaint on the basis of her relationship with the commanding officer. Mrs Graham was consequently transferred to another division. Despite the post providing the same pay and
status, Mrs Graham succeeded with claims for indirect sex discrimination, as well as direct and indirect discrimination on the ground of her
marital status. For the purposes of this section we will concentrate on the
discrimination claims in respect of her marital status. The direct discrimination on marital status succeeded, as the evidence showed that the
Chief Constable had treated the applicant less favourably on grounds of
her marital status than he would have treated an unmarried woman of
the same sex. As for indirect discrimination, the tribunal accepted that a
considerably lesser proportion of married officers of the same sex could
comply with the condition in comparison with unmarried officers.

Furthermore, under EU law, discrimination is also prohibited against
a person on grounds of 'marital or family status' (Equal Treatment
Directive (Directive 76/207), Art. 2(1)). It is interesting to note that this
definition found in this directive is broad enough to cover single as well
as married persons.

Discriminatory grounds: sex, race, colour, nationality, ethnic or national origin

As has been mentioned above the SDA extends to discrimination on grounds of sex and marital status (i.e. it protects married persons). The RRA prohibits discrimination against a person on grounds of colour, race, nationality and ethnic or national origin. The difficulty is determining what these terms mean.

In the well known RRA case of *Mandla* v. *Dowell Lee* (1983), HL, concerning a Sikh boy who was refused entry to a private school because he could not comply with the school's uniform requirements as he wore a turban, the House of Lords defined 'ethnic group'. To be regarded as an ethnic group, the group had to regard itself, and be regarded by others, as a distinct community by virtue of certain characteristics. Two were essential: a long, shared history, and a cultural tradition of its own. Other relevant characteristics include either a common geographical origin or descent from a small number of common ancestors; a common language, literature or religion; and/or a sense of being a minority (or oppressed or dominant) group. The House of Lords held, applying these tests, that Sikhs were indeed a distinct racial group.

The Race Directive, which was issued to combat discrimination across a number of grounds, was implemented by the Race Relations Act 1976 (Amendment) Regulations 2000. Unfortunately, the scope of the directive and that of the RRA are not the same: the directive concerns discrimination on the grounds of race, or ethnic or national origin, while the RRA extends to discrimination on the grounds of colour or nationality. Therefore, although the 2003 regulations amend the RRA in a number of respects, the amendments do not apply to discrimination on the grounds of colour or nationality, which is unsatisfactory and makes the application of the RRA even more complex.

Direct discrimination

Direct discrimination is defined in the SDA and RRA as less favourable treatment on the ground of sex, marital status or gender reassignment (SDA, s. 1(1)(a), 3(1)(a), and 2A(1)(a)), or on racial grounds (RRA, s. 1(1)(a)).

The motive of the discriminator is irrelevant. *James* v. *Eastleigh Borough Council* (1990) involved a married couple, Mr and Mrs James, who were both aged sixty-one. The problem arose when the couple visited a local authority swimming pool. Mrs James gained free admission, whereas Mr James did not, since he had not reached the State pension age of sixty-five. There was no intention to discriminate on the part of the council, it was merely giving concessions to pensioners, under which Mr James did not qualify owing to the different State pension rules for men and women. Mr James contended that this was direct discrimination based solely on the grounds of sex.

The council had no intention to discriminate in this case (in fact, just the opposite!) but the House of Lords held that the test in cases of direct discrimination is objective: the 'but for' test was applied: i.e. but for the complainant's sex, would they have been treated less favourably? The answer here was 'no', so there had been direct discrimination. The intention or motive of the discriminator was irrelevant to that issue. The case also establishes that the application of a discriminatory criterion constitutes direct discrimination.

Less favourable treatment requires a comparison to be carried out. The complainant must be treated by the employer less favourably than a man is treated or would be treated (under the SDA) or a person not of the same race (under the RRA) emphasis. This means that an actual or a hypothetical comparator may be used. This requirement to find an appropriate comparator has caused particular problems when considering pregnancy-related discrimination claims (see below).

Less favourable treatment alone is insufficient to found a claim: the complainant must go on to show that he or she has suffered a detriment (which means being put at a disadvantage): SDA, s. 6(2)(b); RRA, s. 4(2)(c). Often, it is not difficult to find that the complainant has been put at a disadvantage, e.g. by not being appointed to the post applied for, by not getting the promotion or transfer, etc. One particular problem with finding a detriment is whether the test is objective or subjective, i.e. should the individual's views be considered, or should the test be whether a reasonable worker would consider that they had suffered a detriment? In *Shamoon* v. *Chief Constable of the Royal Ulster Constabulary* (2003), the House of Lords held that the latter was the correct approach. Further, it was not necessary to find an economic or physical disadvantage to find a detriment: the detriment in *Shamoon* arose when a police inspector was relieved of the duty of conducting annual appraisals with junior officers.

Harassment

Sexual and racial harassment constitutes direct discrimination, being a form of detriment based on the prohibited grounds. The SDA contains no definition of harassment and has not yet been amended so as to insert express reference to harassment (as is required by the Equal Treatment Amendment Directive (Directive 2003/73/EC).

Vicarious liability of employers

Employers may be liable for acts of harassment committed by employees in the course of their employment (SDA, s. 41; RRA, s. 32). The test to determine whether an act was done 'in the course of employment' is not that used in the law of tort. In *Jones* v. *Tower Boot Co. Ltd* (1997), the Court of Appeal held that the statutory test was distinct from the common law one, i.e. the words 'in the course of employment'. This concept has been stretched to include acts of sexual harassment taking place outside working hours and away from the employer's premises in a social setting (drinks after work): see *Chief Constable of Lincolnshire Police* v. *Stubbs* (1999) in which the EAT held that this was an 'extension' of employment. This would seem to stretch the scope of employers' liability under the statute in a way which leaves them very vulnerable.

Racial harassment

The Race Directive contains provisions relating to harassment, and changes have been made to the RRA by the Race Relations Act 1976 (Amendment) Regulations 2003 (SI 2003/1626). The effect of the regulations is to insert a new s. 3A(1) into the RRA. Harassment occurs where, on the grounds of race or ethnic or national origins, a person engages in unwanted conduct which has the purpose or effect of (1) violating a person's dignity, or (2) creating an intimidating, hostile, degrading, humiliating or offensive environment for him. There are both objective and subjective elements to the definition because conduct is to be regarded as having that effect 'only if, having regard to all the circumstances, including in particular the perception of that other person, it should reasonably be considered as having that effect'. The new definition applies only to harassment on grounds of race or ethnic or national origin.

Sexual harassment

There is currently no express provision in the SDA concerning sexual harassment, although such complaints are brought under ss. 1(1)(a) and

6(2)(b), the latter concerning subjecting a person to a detriment. As sexual harassment is a form of direct discrimination, being less favourable treatment on the ground of sex, it is necessary to establish that (1) the treatment was on this ground (see *Porcelli* v. *Strathclyde Regional Council* (1986) and (2) that the complainant has suffered a detriment judged from the recipient's perspective (see *Shamoon* above and *Wileman* v. *Minilec Engineering Ltd* (1988). A single act of harassment, if it is sufficiently serious, may amount to harassment. See *Bracebridge Engineering Ltd* v. *Darby* (1990) for an example of an outrageous act of discrimination. However, a series of incidents, no one of which taken on its own amounting to harassment, may be sufficient (see *Reed* v. *Stedman* (1999)).

Indirect discrimination

Indirect discrimination is the application of an apparently gender-neutral or race-neutral requirement which places persons of one sex or persons of one colour, racial group, ethnic or national origins at a disadvantage, and which cannot be objectively justified. Essentially, the indirect discrimination provisions concern disparate impact. The relevant provisions concerning the employment field are contained in the SDA, s. 1(2)(b) and the RRA, s. 1(1A). The SDA, s. 1(2)(b), as amended by Sex Discrimination (Indirect Discrimination and Burden of Proof) Regulations (SI 2001/2660) reg. 3, provides that:

a person discriminates against a woman if —

(b)   he applies to her a provision, criterion or practice which he applies or would apply equally to a man but —

   (i)   which is such that it would be to the detriment of a considerably larger proportion of women than of men, and
   (ii) which he cannot show to be justifiable irrespective of the sex of the person to whom it is applied, and
   (iii) which is to her detriment.

In *Price* v. *Civil Service Commission* (1978), for example, it was an age requirement for a civil service post. The successful applicant had to be between seventeen and twenty-eight. The complainant, who was thirty-two, succeeded in her claim that this was indirect sex discrimination, as it disadvantaged women, who would be more likely to be over this age as they often took time out of their career for childbirth and child rearing.

Victimisation

Victimisation is a form of direct discrimination, i.e. it is less favourable treatment of a person by reason that they have brought proceedings, given evidence or information, or alleged a contravention of the SDA, RRA or EqPA (the 'protected acts') or where the discriminator knows or suspects that that the person victimised intends to do any of those things, or suspects the person has done, or intends to do, any of them (SDA, s. 4; RRA, s 2).

The allegation by the person victimised must be true and made in good faith. The alleged motive of the discriminator is not relevant – indeed, it may be unconscious or subconscious (*Nagarajan* v. *London Regional Transport* (1999), HL: a case where the complainant was not appointed to a position because he had made claims against the employer before under the RRA). The House of Lords held that the protected act need not be the only reason for the treatment it is sufficient if it is a substantial reason. In *Chief Constable of West Yorkshire Police* v. *Khan* (2001), HL, the House of Lords held that the correct comparison was with someone who had not performed a protected act. Victimisation is established if the person has been treated less favourably *by reason* that he has performed such an act. In *Khan*, their lordships held that it was the existence of proceedings brought by Mr Khan which meant that they could not supply the reference he requested for the purpose of a job application he had made to another police force, as this might prejudice those proceedings. The decision in *Khan* seems difficult to reconcile with the House of Lords in *Nagarajan*.

DISABILITY DISCRIMINATION

Legislation concerning discrimination on the ground of disability has been on the statute book for some time. However, the Disabled Persons (Employment) Act 1944 required a person with a sufficient degree of disability to register so that the quota system could operate, i.e. employers with twenty or more employees were required to employ a quota (3 per cent) of disabled persons. This scheme was not successful because there were no civil remedies for breach of the provision; employers evaded the quota scheme by securing blanket permits allowing them to employ able-bodied employees (their argument was that there were no suitably qualified disabled persons for the job); and only about a third of those disabled registered under the scheme. The Act was replaced by the Disability Discrimination Act 1995 (the DDA).

The DDA covers discrimination against disabled persons in employment (Part II of the Act) and in relation to the provision of goods, services and facilities (Part III), although this discussion considers the former. Part II of the DDA was brought into force on 1 December 1996. In 1996, in addition to the main statute, two sets of regulations were brought into force, the Disability Discrimination (Meaning of Disability) Regulations 1996 (SI 1996 No. 1455), and the Disability Discrimination (Employment) Regulations 1996 (SI 1996 No. 1456). The Secretary of State has also issued guidance, pursuant to powers under DDA, s. 3: ('the Guidance'), and a Code of Practice giving practical guidance on matters relating to the elimination of disability discrimination in employment, encouraging good employment practices in relation to the disabled, and on reasonable adjustments. The EAT has stated that employment tribunals should make express reference to the code in their decisions (see *Ridout* v. *TC Group* (1998); *Goodwin* v. *Patent Office* (1999)). The Court of Appeal has held that, when determining whether there has been less favourable treatment, the relevant provisions of the code should be taken into account (*Clark* v. *Novacold* (1999)).

As is the case in the SDA and the RRA, the DDA applies to employees, i.e. those working under a contract of employment or apprenticeship, and those who work under 'a contract personally to do any work' (DDA, s. 68). It includes employees and contract workers (new ss. 4 and 4B). The employment provisions of the DDA apply to work in an establishment in Great Britain. Since 1 October 2004 employees not previously covered by the Act, e.g. police officers, fire-fighters, partnerships, barristers and prison officers have been within the scope of the Act's employment provisions (armed forces members will continue to be excluded) (DDA, ss. 6A, 7A, 64, 64A).

The DDA, s. 4(2), as originally drafted, did not cover discrimination against former employees: it concerned discrimination by employers against a person 'whom he employs'. From 1 October 2004 coverage was extended to ex-employees (see the Amendment Regulations (SI 2003/1673) reg. 15, which insert a new s. 16A in the DDA).

Meaning of disability

The relevant definitions relating to 'disability' and 'disabled person' are set out in the DDA, s. 1 and Sch. 1. The DDA takes the 'medical model', rather than the 'social model', of disability. Essentially, medical evidence determines whether a person is disabled. Application of the social model would mean that a person may be seen as suffering discrimination because they are perceived to be disabled.

A person has a disability for the purposes of the DDA if he has a physical or mental impairment which has a substantial and long-term adverse effect on his or her ability to carry out normal day-to-day activities. S. 2 includes in the definition of a 'disabled person' a person who has had a disability. This covers situations were someone with a past disability who is no longer suffering any effects may still be discriminated against. The key points to note about this definition are:

1 A person must have a *physical or mental impairment.*
2 That impairment must have an *adverse effect* on his or her *ability to carry out normal day-to-day activities.*
3 That effect must be *substantial.*
4 That effect must also be *long-term.*

Mental impairments include learning, psychiatric and psychological impairments. If the impairment results from or consists of a mental illness, it must be clinically well recognised to come within the definition (Sch. 1, para. 1(1)). However, psychopathic or antisocial disorders (e.g. kleptomania, pryomania and paedophilia) were originally excluded in 1995 (reg. 4(1)). Spectacle wearers and hay-fever sufferers are also outside the definition of disability.

'Normal day-to-day activities' (not necessarily those concerning the job the employee is or will be doing) must be affected, i.e.:

1 mobility;
2 manual dexterity;

3   physical co-ordination;
4   continence;
5   ability to lift, carry or otherwise move everyday objects;
6   speech, hearing or eyesight;
7   memory or ability to concentrate, learn or understand; or
8   perception of the risk of physical danger.

Sch. 1, para. 4(1)

SEXUAL ORIENTATION; RELIGION OR BELIEF

Despite the fact that there has been discrimination legislation at domestic level concerning sex and race since the middle of the 1970s, there has been a gap concerning other grounds of discrimination, i.e. sexual orientation, religion or belief and age (with disability not being addressed until 1995 under the DDA). Impetus for change came once again from the European Union with the introduction under the Amsterdam Treaty in 1997 of a new Article 13 to be incorporated in the Treaty of Rome. This empowered the EU's Council of Ministers to take action to combat discrimination across a wide area: sex, racial or ethnic origin, religion or belief, disability, age or sexual orientation. The European Union used this power to adopt the Equal Treatment Framework Directive (2000/781 EC), which required Member States to legislate against these forms of discrimination by 2003, with the exception of age and disability, for which the implementation date is 2006.

As a result of the directive, two sets of regulations were adopted: the Employment Equality (Sexual Orientation) Regulations 2003 (SI 2003/1661), which came into force on 1 December 2003 and the Employment Equality (Religion or Belief) Regulations 2003 (SI 2003/1660), which came into force on 2 December 2003.

Sexual orientation

Until 2003 there was no protection in Great Britain concerning discrimination on the ground of sexual orientation. The SDA makes unlawful discrimination 'on the ground of sex', whereas gay and lesbian complainants were bringing claims under the SDA on the ground of sexual orientation.

The courts and tribunals took a restrictive view: the SDA requires a comparison between the complainant and an actual or hypothetical comparator of the *opposite sex*, so that the complainant would succeed only where it could be established that an actual or hypothetical person of the opposite sex but with the same sexual orientation, i.e. homosexuality, would not have been treated less favourably. Where such a comparator would have been treated in the same way as the complainant, i.e. badly, there was no contravention of the SDA. Thus, in *Pearce* v. *Governing Body of Mayfield Secondary School* (2003), a case concerning homophobic abuse by pupils of a female teacher who was lesbian, the House of Lords held that this was not direct sex discrimination, as a male homosexual teacher would have been subjected to such abuse (see also *Smith* v. *Gardner Merchant Ltd* (1998)). The acts complained of in *Pearce* took place before the coming into force of the Human Rights Act 1998 on 2 October 1998, so no claim could be brought on the basis of an infringement of human rights.

Employment Equality (Religion and Belief) Regulations 2003

The Employment Equality (Religion and Belief) Regulations 2003 (SI 2003/1660) are drafted in similar terms to the SO Regs, with the relevant changes being made. The four forms of discrimination rendered unlawful are direct, indirect, harassment and victimisation. Thus, for direct discrimination, the definition is less favourable treatment on the grounds of religion or belief, while indirect discrimination involves (1) the application by A of a provision, criterion or practice which he applies or would apply to persons not of the same religion or belief as B, but (2) which puts or would put persons of the same religion or belief as B at a particular disadvantage when compared with other persons, (3) which puts B at that disadvantage, and (4) which cannot be shown to be a proportionate means of achieving a legitimate aim (reg. 3). The religion or belief must not be that of A (reg. 3(2)).

It should be noted that, in direct discrimination, the less favourable treatment must be on 'grounds of religion or belief', which does not necessarily have to be that of the complainant. For example, the definition could apply to an individual (X) who fraternises with or supports another person (Y), whether financially or in other ways, but who does not share Y's religion or belief, who is discriminated against because of that fraternisation or support of Y.

DEFENCES TO DISCRIMINATION CLAIMS

To determine whether the objective justification found in Article 141 of the Treaty on the European Union has been established the test laid down in *Bilka* must be satisfied. The ECJ in *Bilka* ruled that in order to justify the provision that is being questioned as discriminatory the employer must show that the condition:

1 corresponds to a real need on the part of the employer;
2 is appropriate with a view to achieving the objective pursued;
3 is necessary to achieving that end result.

The objective approach in *Bilka* was followed in *Hampson* v. *Department of Education and Science* (1989) where the Court of Appeal rejected the employer's justification defence that the complainant's qualifications as a teacher in Hong Kong were not comparable to those required in the United Kingdom. The court held that an objective balance needs to be struck between the discriminatory effect of the provision and the employer's legitimate business needs. The ECJ's ruling in *R* v. *Secretary of State for Employment,* ex parte *Seymour-Smith and Perez* (1999) and the House of Lords' decision in *R* v. *Secretary of State for Employement,* ex parte *Seymour-Smith and Perez (No. 2)* (2000), where the House of Lords held that the qualification period for unfair dismissal rights of part-timers, which was then two years, was objectively justifiable.

Genuine occupational qualification

Where sex or race is a genuine occupational qualification (GOQ) for the job, less favourable treatment will be allowed (SDA, s. 7; RRA, s. 5). This exception comprises a fairly narrow range of reasons, e.g. under SDA, s. 7(2):

1   where the essential nature of the job calls for a man for reasons of physiology (excluding physical strength or stamina) or, in dramatic performances or other entertainment, for reasons of authenticity, so that the essential nature of the job would be materially different if carried out by a woman;

2   the job needs to be held by a man to preserve decency or privacy because:

   (a)   it is likely to involve physical contact with men in circumstances where they might reasonably object to its being carried out by a woman, or

   (b)   the holder of the job is likely to do his work in circumstances where men might reasonably object to the presence of a woman because they are in a state of undress or are using sanitary facilities.

3   The job is likely to involve the holder of the job doing his work, or living, in a private home and needs to be held by a man because objection might reasonably be taken to allowing a woman –

   (a)   the degree of physical or social contact with a person living in the home, or

   (b)   the knowledge of intimate details of such a person's life, which is likely, because of the nature or circumstances of the job, or of the home, to be allowed to, or available to, the holder of the job.

Justification in disability discrimination claims

Before it was amended the DDA allowed a justification defence for failure to make reasonable adjustments under s. 5. The Amendment Regulations have amended the DDA in this regard by repealing that provision and substituting a new s. 3A (in force from 1 October 2004) which provides that, apart from direct discrimination (see s. 3A(4)), discriminatory treatment may be justified where the reason for it is both 'material to the circumstances of the particular case and substantial'. However, the pre-amendment case law will continue to be of importance. This establishes that the standard to be applied when considering the justification is the objective one, meaning that the Employment Tribunal must come to its own conclusion on the matter, considering whether (under the new amended DDA) on the facts of the case reasonable adjustments could be made. (The pre-amendment case law concerns direct discrimination, or more specifically less favourable treatment, as well as the duty to make reasonable adjustments.) If it decides that there were reasonable adjustments that could be made, then it must consider whether the employer was reasonable in not carrying them out (see *Morse* v. *Wiltshire County Council* (1998), EAT). According to the Court of Appeal in *Jones* v. *Post Office* (2001), the test is akin to that applied by employment tribunals when considering whether a dismissal was unfair; thus the band of reasonable responses test is the test to be applied.

Complaints under the DDA are to be made to the employment tribunal within three months of the act complained of (s. 17A). The tribunal may make a declaration, or an order for compensation (which is unlimited, and may include a sum for injury to feelings), or a recommendation to the respondent. Compensation can be very high in disability cases. For example, over £100,000 was awarded to the complainant in *British Sugar* v. *Kirker* (1998), EAT.

REMEDIES

An individual may make an application to an employment tribunal within three months of the alleged act of discrimination, although the tribunal may extend this where it considers it is just and equitable to do so (SDA, s. 76; RRA, s. 68). The EOC and the CRE have the power to assist applicants where the case raises matters of principle or it is unreasonable to expect the applicant to deal with the case without support (SDA, s. 75; RRA, s. 66).

If the complaint is upheld, the tribunal may: (1) make an order declaring the rights of the parties; (2) award compensation (which is unlimited); (3) make a recommendation that the employer takes action within a specified period to obviate or reduce the effect of the discrimination (SDA, s. 65(1); RRA, s. 56(1)(a)). On recommendations, see *British Gas* v. *Sharma* (1991); *North West Thames Regional Health Authority* v. *Noone* (1988), where ETs required employers to modify their policies.

Compensation for injury to feelings may be awarded, and often comprises a major part of the compensation (SDA, s. 66(4); RRA, s. 57(4)). The statutory cap on compensation in discrimination was removed in 1993 following the ECJ's ruling in *Marshall* v. *Southampton and South West Hampshire Area Health Authority (No. 2)* (1993), in which the statutory limits were held to be in breach of the Community law requirement that domestic remedies were adequate for a breach of Community law. The Sex Discrimination and Equal Pay (Remedies) Regulations 1993 (SI 1993/ 2798) removed the statutory cap on compensation for sex discrimination, and the RRA was amended by the Race Relations (Remedies) Act 1994, which abolished the statutory limit on compensation in race discrimination cases.

INTERACTIVE LEARNING

1 Prakash and Hari are Sikhs. Winston, aged twenty seven, is black, of West Indian origin, and came to England five years ago. Vacancies for jobs on the production line at Quick Snacks' factory are advertised in the local press. A written application and four passes at GCSE level are required for applicants. Prakash has difficulty writing English and asks a friend to complete the application form. Quick Snacks' board of directors decides as a matter of policy to reject all Sikh applicants: employees in the personnel office who process the application are duly informed of this and instructed to comply with the board's decision. Prakash and Hari's applications are rejected, as is Winston's, on the ground that he does not have the required GCSE passes. Robert, a clerical worker in the human resources department, informs the Commission for Racial Equality about the board's policy. When his manager discovers this, Robert is summarily dismissed. Advise Prakash, Hari and Winston.

2 List the remedies available for discrimination cases. Assess the significance of each for the employer.

3 What powers do the EOC, CRE and DRC have in discrimination cases?

6

Family Rights

MATERNITY RIGHTS

Women have four rights in relation to pregnancy and childbirth. These are: the right to maternity leave; the right to maternity pay; time off for antenatal care; and protection from detriment or dismissal on the grounds of pregnancy or childbirth. The Pregnant Workers Directive 92/85/EEC required Member States to provide women workers with at least fourteen weeks' maternity leave. The relevant domestic law is now contained within Regulations 71–5 and the Maternity and Parental Leave etc. Regulations 1999, SI 1999/3312, as amended by the Maternity and Parental Leave (Amendment) Regulations 2002 (SI 2002/2789) (MPLAR 2002), which apply to mothers of children born on or after 6 April 2003.

Ordinary maternity leave

Women are entitled to a period of ordinary maternity leave (OML) of twenty-six weeks (without the need to accrue a qualifying period of continuous employment): MPLR, reg. 7.

There are detailed notification requirements to be followed, failing which the maternity leave may be lost. The employee must notify her employer no later than the end of the fifteenth week before the expected week of childbirth (EWC) – or as soon as reasonably practicable – of the fact that she is pregnant, the expected date of childbirth and the date on which she intends to commence her OML (reg. 4). This date may be varied by notifying the employer at least twenty-eight days before the date varied or before the new date, whichever is the earlier. The employer must then give the woman notice of the date on which her OML will end (reg. 8). If the employer fails to do this she may return early, and she is protected from detriment or dismissal if she does not return on that date (regs 10(c), 13 and 14).

After her OML a woman has the right to return to the job in which she was employed before her absence, on terms no less favourable than she would have enjoyed had she not been absent (reg. 18).

Unfair dismissal and protection from detriment

A woman is protected from detriment for exercising or seeking to exercise her right to maternity leave, and it is an automatically unfair dismissal to dismiss a woman for a reason connected with pregnancy, childbirth or maternity leave rights (regs 19 and 20). There is one exception to this provision on automatically unfair dismissal: it is not automatically unfair to dismiss a woman (for a reason other than redundancy) if it is not reasonably practicable to allow her to return to a suitable job and she has accepted or unreasonably refused the offer of such a job made by an associated employer (reg. 20(7)).

Additional maternity leave

A woman who is entitled to OML and who has been continuously employed for a period of twenty-six weeks by the fourteenth week before the EWC is entitled to a period of additional maternity leave (AML) of twenty six weeks (regs 5 and 7). This gives qualifying female employees a total maternity leave entitlement of one year. However, maternity leave only attracts statutory maternity pay for the first twenty-six weeks of leave (see the section on statutory maternity pay), which means that, in practice, women will wish to take the full fifty-two weeks of leave only if there is a contractual entitlement covering the last half of the leave year. The woman returning from AML has the same right as relates to OML to return to the job in which she was employed before her absence, on terms no less favourable than she would have enjoyed had she not been absent (reg. 18).

Statutory maternity pay

A woman with twenty-six weeks of continuous employment by the fifteenth week before the EWC with average earnings at or above the lower earnings limit (£85 per week from 6 April 2005) for the payment of National Insurance contributions is entitled to statutory maternity pay (SMP): see the Social Security Contributions and Benefits Act 1992, ss. 164–71. For the first six weeks it is paid at the rate of 90 per cent of the woman's normal weekly earnings. For the remaining twenty weeks it is paid at the rate of statutory sick pay, which from April 2005 is £108 per week. A woman must give twenty-eight days' notice of the day SMP should start.

Time off for antenatal care

A pregnant employee may request paid time off work to attend an antenatal appointment, which the employer may not unreasonably refuse. The employer may request written proof of the pregnancy and the appointment (ERA, ss. 55 and 56). The amount of pay is the normal hourly rate. The employee may complain to an employment tribunal that her employer has unreasonably refused time off or has failed to pay her for the time off. The tribunal may make a declaration and order the amount of pay due. Dismissal or subjection to a detriment because the employee has exercised her right under these provisions will give her the right to claim under the MPLR, regs 19 and 20, as well to complain of unfair dismissal (as well as sex discrimination). Table 6.1 summarises maternity rights.

PATERNITY LEAVE

The Employment Act 2002 (EA 2002), s. 1, introduced new rights to paternity leave (PL) by inserting new sections into the ERA, ss. 80A and 80B (in force from 8 December 2002). These concern the two categories of paternity leave: one concerning the birth of a child (called 'paternity leave: birth'), and the other concerning adoption (called 'paternity leave: adoption'). Although the provisions relating to these two categories are similar, there are some differences and the two forms of paternity leave are treated separately below. Under the ERA, s. 1, the Secretary of State

Table 6.1   Maternity rights of a pregnant worker summarised

Ordinary maternity leave (OML)	Additional maternity leave (AML)	Statutory maternity pay	Antenatal care rights
Up to twenty six weeks, providing the correct notice is given.	Up to twenty six weeks, so long as she has been continuously employed for twenty six weeks by the fourteenth week before the expected birth date.	Only entitled to this payment in respect of OML. This is set at 90% of normal weekly earnings for the first six weeks, and at the rate of statutory sick pay for the remaining twenty. To qualify, average earnings must reach the lower earnings limit for NI contributions.	Request may be made for paid time off to attend antenatal classes. The employee's normal hourly rate applies. This request cannot be unreasonably refused.

was given power to make regulations concerning paternity leave, which was done by making the Paternity and Adoption Leave Regulations 2002 (SI 2002/2788) (PALR), which came into force on 8 December 2002. Where there is also a contractual right to paternity leave an employee may not operate both rights separately but may choose whichever right is more favourable, i.e. he may choose either the contractual right or the statutory one, but not both (PALR, reg. 30). Furthermore, paternity leave is in addition to the thirteen weeks' *parental* leave entitlement, discussed above.

The PALR apply to fathers of children born on or after 6 April 2003 and who have been continuously employed for not less than twenty-six weeks ending with the week immediately preceding the fourteenth week before the expected week of the child's birth. However, it should be noted that the interpretation of 'partner' in regulation 2, which defines a partner as 'a person (whether of a different or the same sex) who lives with the mother ... and the child in an enduring family relationship but is not a relative of the mother ...' is clearly broad enough for the purposes of regulation 4(2) – discussed below – to apply to a *woman*, despite the fact that it is called *paternity* leave. This means, for example, the right to paternity leave could also apply (if the requirements set out in regs 2 and 4 are met) to the female partner of a woman in a lesbian relationship where that woman has had a child. However, the masculine form will be used in this description of the PALR, which should be read as also importing the feminine.

The entitlement is up to two weeks' paid leave, which must be taken together – there is no right to take separate days of leave, although an employee may choose to take either one week's leave or two consecutive weeks' leave – and it must be taken within fifty-six days of the birth (PALR, reg. 5(2)). The employee is entitled to Statutory Paternity Pay (SPP), which is paid at the same rate as SMP. With effect from 6 April 2005, this is £108 per week, or 90 per cent of average weekly earnings if this is less than that sum. These figures normally change every year (see: EA 2002, s. 7; Statutory Paternity Pay and Statutory Adoption Pay (General) Regulations 2002 (SI 2002/2822), reg. 3; and the Statutory Paternity Pay and Statutory Adoption Pay (Weekly Rates) Regulations 2002 (SI 2002/2818), reg. 2. As with SMP, there are recoupment provisions which mean that employers can recover SPP paid to employees, which from April, 2004 is at the rate of 92 per cent for large employers and 104.5 per cent for small employers, i.e. those with a National Insurance liability (from April 2004) of £45,000 or less (see the Statutory Paternity Pay and Statutory Adoption Pay (Administration) Regulations 2002 (SI 2002/2820), reg. 3).

The PALR also contains provisions on paternity leave for employees on the adoption of a child, defined as a person who is under eighteen when placed for adoption. (It is important to note that this right is not to be confused with *adoption leave*, which is discussed below.) Many of the provisions concerning paternity leave relating to adoption are similar to those governing paternity leave on the birth of a child, e.g. those on qualifying for the entitlement, the period of leave allowed and the requirement that it must be taken within fifty-six days of (in this case) the date on which the child is placed with the adopter (PALR, regs 8 and 9(2)). The declaration requirements are also similar. However, the notice requirements differ from those relating to paternity leave: birth. Employees must give their employer notice of their intention to take this form of PL no more than seven days after the date on which the adopter is notified of having been matched with the child.

PARENTAL LEAVE

The major impetus for the introduction of a right to parental leave came from the European Union. During the 1980s and early 1990s the United

Kingdom vetoed proposals from the Commission concerning parental leave (whether paid or unpaid). The other Member States adopted the procedure set out in the Social Policy Protocol under which they could adopt social policy legislation without the United Kingdom blocking such moves.

The Parental Leave Directive actually requires the implementation of two 'family-friendly' rights:

1   the right to leave to care for young children (up to eight years of age, according to Clause 2(1) of the Directive;
2   the right to time off work to care for dependants in family emergencies.

This section deals with the former right, while the latter is considered in a subsequent section.

Under the MPLR, both male and female employees, whether full-time or part-time, are entitled to *unpaid* parental leave of up to thirteen weeks (per parent, per child) if they have one year's continuous employment and have (or expect to have) responsibility for the child (MPLR, regs 2 and 13(1)(a)(b), 14(1)). An employee has responsibility for a child where he or she has 'parental responsibility' (as defined in the Children Act 1989, s. 3 – a definition which is broad enough to include an adopted child) or where they have been registered as the parent on the child's birth certificate. There is a separate entitlement for each parent. The period of thirteen weeks' leave must be taken in periods of a week or multiples of a week, except for parents of disabled children, who may take leave of a day or multiples of a day (the limitations of this provision are discussed below) during the first five years of the child's life or, in the case of an adopted child, within five years of the placement for adoption or the child's eighteenth birthday, whichever is the earlier (MPLR, regs 14(1), 15, Sch. 2, para. 7). This maximum leave period is extended to eighteen weeks in the case of employees with a child who are entitled to disability living allowance (MPLR, reg. 14(1A)). The leave is 'for the purpose of caring for that child' (MPLR reg. 13(1)).

Employers and employees may make their own agreements on how to implement the parental leave right by adopting individual, collective or workforce agreements. This would allow them to agree, for example, that parental leave could be taken in units of less than one week, e.g. one day, which may be more convenient for the employee. In the absence of such an agreement, the default provisions apply (Schedule 2).

Employees must give at least twenty-one days' notice of their intention to take parental leave (MPLR, Sch. 2, para. 1). In the case of employees giving such notice before the expected week of childbirth or placement for adoption, the employer must allow the leave. Apart from those two situations, the employer may postpone it for up to six months where he 'considers that the operation of his business would be unduly disrupted' if the employee took the leave, giving the employee seven days' notice in writing of the postponement (MPLR, Sch. 2, para. 6). An employee may complain to an employment tribunal that the employer has unreasonably postponed a period of parental leave or prevented or attempted to prevent him from taking it (ERA, s. 80).

Under regulation 17 the employee is entitled to certain terms and conditions of employment which apply during the period of parental leave, apart from the right to pay. These are: the implied term of trust and confidence; notice of termination of the contract; compensation upon redundancy; and the disciplinary and grievance procedures. During leave, the employee is bound by the implied obligation of good faith and any terms relating to: notice of termination; disclosure of confidential information; the acceptance of gifts or other benefits; or participation in any business.

Employees returning after parental leave of four weeks or less are entitled to return to the job they were doing before going on leave. Employees taking longer periods of leave are entitled to return to the job they were doing before going on leave or, where that is not reasonably practicable, to a suitable and appropriate job (MPLR, reg. 18). Upon return, the employee's right to remuneration, seniority, pension rights and other similar rights must be no less favourable than they were before taking leave (reg. 18A).

FLEXIBLE WORKING

In November 2001 the DTI's Work and Parents Task Force produced a report proposing that employees who were parents of children under six should be able to request flexible working arrangements, and that the employer should be required to take the request seriously. This was taken up by the government, and a provision was inserted into the ERA by the Employment Act 2002 (see ERA, ss. 80F–I), effective from 6 April 2003. There are two sets of regulations on flexible working: the Flexible

Working (Procedural Requirements) Regulations 2002 (SI 2002/3207) and the Flexible Working (Eligibility, Complaints and Remedies) Regulations 2002 (SI 2002/3236). The right is to *request* to work flexibly (i.e. a right to request a contractual variation), rather than an automatic right to do so. The change must relate to hours or times and place of work (ERA, s. 80F(1)(a)).

To qualify for this right, the employee must :

1 be a qualifying employee, i.e. with at least twenty-six weeks of continuous employment (reg. 3(1)(a);
2 have or expect to have responsibility for the upbringing of a child aged under six (or under eighteen if the child is disabled): ERA, s. 80F(3) and (7);
3 be either the parent, foster parent, guardian, or adopter of the child, or the husband, wife or partner of such a person (reg. 3(1)(b)).

The employer must hold a meeting within twenty-eight days of the request, and inform the employee of the decision within fourteen days of the meeting (regs 3 and 4). The employee may be accompanied by a fellow worker. The employee may appeal against the decision within fourteen days and, if an appeal is made, an appeal meeting must be held within fourteen days of the appeal being lodged, unless the appeal is upheld within fourteen days of the appeal being lodged (regs 6 and 8).

Grounds for refusal

The employer may refuse the request only on 'business grounds' (ERA, s. 80G(1)(b)). These are:

1 burden of additional costs;
2 detrimental effect on the ability to meet customer demand;
3 inability to reorganise work among existing staff;
4 inability to recruit additional staff;
5 detrimental impact on quality or performance;
6 insufficiency of work during periods that the employee proposes to work planned structural changes;
7 any other ground that the Secretary of State may specify.

TIME OFF FOR DEPENDANTS

The Parental Leave Directive required Member States to introduce the right for workers to take time off for urgent family reasons. This was implemented by inserting a provision into the ERA, s. 57A (as amended by the Employment Relations Act 1999), giving employees a statutory right to request time off to care for dependants. No qualifying period of employment is necessary for entitlement to the right. A 'dependant' is the employee's wife, husband, child, parent or someone living in the same household (but is not his or her employee, tenant, lodger or boarder (ERA, s. 57A(3)). This is broad enough to include partners of the opposite or the same sex as the employee. The definition also includes a person who reasonably relies on the employee for assistance when they fall ill, are injured or assaulted, or who relies on the employee to make arrangements for the provision of care in the event of illness or injury (ERA, s. 57A(4)). Where there is unexpected disruption or termination of arrangements for the care of a dependant, the definition also includes any person who reasonably relies on the employee to make arrangements for care (ERA, s. 57A(5)).

PART-TIME WORKERS

Encouraging part-time work and providing the opportunity to switch from full-time to part-time working, and ensuring adequate employment protection for those wishing to do so, is a very important aspect of achieving a better work/life balance across the labour market. The protections introduced for part-time workers may thus be seen as part of the package of family-friendly policies. The EC Part-time Work Directive 97/81/EC of 5 December 1997 (which was extended to apply to the United Kingdom by the Part-time Workers Directive, 98/23EC) was implemented by the Part-time Workers (Prevention of Less Favourable Treatment) Regulations 2000 (SI 2000/1551) (PTWR) on 1 July 2000, some three months after the implementation date of 7 April 2000. The DTI has issued detailed guidance, *Part-time Workers: The Law and Best Practice*, which encourages employers to afford opportunities for allowing workers to switch to part-time work, and to consider more flexible working. This is in line with the objectives of the directive, although the guidance does not have legal force.

Regulation 5(2) provides that:

A part-time worker has the right not to be treated by his employer less favourably than the employer treats a comparable full-time worker –

(a)   as regards the terms of his contract; or
(b)   by being subjected to any other detriment by any act, or deliberate failure to act, of his employer'.

Pro rata principle

Part-time workers are entitled to the same treatment *pro rata* as full-timers doing similar work unless the less favourable treatment can be objectively justified. For the purposes of this chapter, which focuses on family-friendly policies, it is important to note that part-timers must have the same entitlement to maternity leave (and maternity pay), parental leave, and time off for dependants, on a *pro rata* basis, as comparable full-time workers (PTWR, reg. 5).

Objective justification

The right of a part-timer not to be treated less favourably than a comparable full-timer applies only if the treatment cannot be justified on objective grounds. Justification of the less favourable treatment on objective grounds means that it must be shown that it:

1   is to achieve a legitimate objective, for example, a genuine business objective;
2   is necessary to achieve that objective; and
3   is an appropriate way to achieve the objective.

INTERACTIVE LEARNING

1   Legally define what is meant by the term 'family-friendly'. What legal obligations does it give rise to?
2   Consider the following case: *British Airways (European Operations at Gatwick) Ltd* v. *Moore* (2000). M and B both became pregnant during the course of their employment as pursers with British Airways.

(Continued)

(Continued)

- Under their terms and conditions of employment they could no longer be employed on flying duties after their sixteenth week of pregnancy.
- They accepted alternative work in ground posts.
- Basic pay remained the same but they lost out on flying allowances that they had previously enjoyed.
- M and B claimed (a) unlawful deduction from wages; (b) breach of right to remuneration on suspension on maternity grounds; (c) breach of the Equal Pay Act 1970; (d) unlawful sex discrimination.

Advise the tribunal on:

(a)   Whether the claim for unlawful deductions should succeed.

(b)   If M and B were not offered *suitable alternative employment* with terms and conditions no less favourable than those they would be entitled to under their normal work, can their remuneration claims succeed?

(c)   Whether M and B's equal pay claims should succeed.

3   Devise a 'flexible work' policy, ensuring that you comply with all the statutory requirements.

7

Termination of Employment

When employees are dismissed they may claim to have been dismissed either:

1   in breach of contract; or
2   in breach of their statutory rights.

A dismissal in breach of contract is usually called a 'wrongful dismissal'. A claim for breach of statutory rights will take the form of either a complaint of unfair dismissal and/or a claim for a statutory redundancy payment. This chapter concentrates on wrongful and constructive dismissal.

DISTINGUISHING WRONGFUL DISMISSAL AND UNFAIR DISMISSAL

The critical distinction between a 'wrongful' and an 'unfair' dismissal lies in the limitations of the law of contract. If a person is dismissed in breach of contract – for example, without the notice to which he or she was entitled under the contract – then the common law is able to intervene and a claim may be made. If, however, the person is dismissed with the notice to which he or she was entitled, the common law can no longer deal with the matter, since there has been no breach of contract. It is at this point that the law of *unfair* dismissal becomes important. The success or otherwise of a statutory claim to have been unfairly dismissed depends not upon whether there has been a breach of contract but upon whether the employer has dismissed the employee in a way which does not infringe his or her statutory rights; in other words, whether the dismissal was fair or unfair. Thus it is perfectly feasible for the situation to exist where an employee is dismissed in accordance with the contract but in a way which contravenes his or her statutory rights. In such a case, a wrongful dismissal claim will fail, whereas an unfair dismissal claim will succeed. It is important to bear in mind that the terms 'unfair' and 'wrongful' cannot be used interchangeably. They are terms of art and embody different legal concepts.

DISMISSAL?

Determining whether a dismissal has in fact taken place, and at what point in time this occured, is often a curious question. However, the examples below may explain it.

Expiry of a fixed-term contract

Fixed-term contracts may take a number of forms. The contract may specify that it is to continue for a stated period (e.g. five years from 1 January 2004). In that case, it cannot be terminated before the expiry of that period, unless its terms empower the parties to terminate it earlier or they agree to bring it to an end. In *Dixon* v. *British Broadcasting Corporation* (1979) the Court of Appeal held that, in the context of employment protection legislation, such a contract is a contract for a fixed term even though it is terminable by notice on either side before the expiry of the term. Lord Denning MR emphasised that a fixed-term contract must be for a specified period.

It should be noted that limitations have been placed on the use of fixed-term contracts by the Fixed-term Employees (Prevention of Less Favourable Treatment) Regulations 2002 (SI 2002/2034). The effect of these regulations is, among other things, to prevent less favourable treatment of fixed-term employees by comparison with permanent employees and to convert fixed-term contracts into permanent contracts in the case of employees continuously employed for four years or more: see regs 3 and 8.

Frustration

Frustration occurs when circumstances beyond the control of either party to a contract make it incapable of being performed in the form which was undertaken by the contracting parties. In that case, the contract will terminate automatically and the frustrating event will not be treated as dismissal for the purposes of any dismissal claim, whether at common law or under the statute.

The doctrine of frustration applies to a contract of employment, the most common examples being illness and imprisonment. The death of either party is also best treated as a frustrating event. The effect of frustration is to terminate the contract automatically without either party having to take steps to bring it to an end.

It is clear that the doctrine of frustration can in appropriate circumstances be applied to a periodic contract terminable by the employer by short notice (see *Notcutt* v. *Universal Equipment Co. (London) Ltd* (1986)). The facts of that case were that the employee, a skilled workman, started working for the employers in 1957 under a contract which was terminable by one week's notice and which provided that no remuneration would be paid to him when he was absent from work because of sickness. In 1983 he suffered a coronary infarct and was absent from work from then on. By July 1984, when the employers were required to give him twelve weeks' notice under what is now ERA 1996, s. 86, it had become apparent that he would never be able to work again. So the employers gave him the requisite twelve weeks' notice. The employee claimed sick pay during the period of his notice, but the county court judge dismissed his claim on the grounds that his contract had been frustrated by illness before the notice was given. The Court of Appeal upheld the decision. It is not clear, however, when the court regarded the contract as having ended. Dillon LJ seems to suggest that it was when the employee had the coronary; Sheldon J said that the latest moment when the frustration could have occurred was when the medical report was presented.

It is not entirely clear whether the imposition of a custodial sentence upon an employee frustrates the contract or terminates it by making it impossible for the employee to perform his or her part of the contract, in terms of the differences of view of the members of the Court of Appeal in *Hare* v. *Murphy Brothers Ltd* (1974). In the later case of *F. C. Shepherd & Co. Ltd* v. *Jerrom* (1986) the Court of Appeal did not follow its decision in that case, which it regarded as unsatisfactory. It decided that a sentence of Borstal training was an event which was not foreseen or provided for by the parties at the time of contracting and that it rendered the performance of the contract radically different from that which the parties had contemplated when they entered into it. There had been no fault or default on the part of the employers and the employee was not entitled to rely on his own default. His criminal conduct, although deliberate, had no effect on the performance of the contract: the imposition of the custodial sentence was the act of the judge. The custodial sentence did frustrate the contract of apprenticeship in this case, since the imposition of the sentence meant that there would be a break in the period of training and at the end of the period of the agreement the employee would not be so well trained as the parties had contemplated he would be. Mustill LJ expressly dealt with the question of self-induced frustration and said that, by asserting that the frustration was self-induced, the employee 'asserts that he himself had repudiated the contract: and this is something which, in my judgement, he should not be allowed to do'.

Mutual consent

At common law the parties are free to enter into an agreement that the contract should terminate. They may also put a clause in the contract by which the employee agrees to accept a stipulated amount in satisfaction of any claims he or she may have in the event of specified events occurring, for example the premature termination of the contract. It is also open to them to agree in advance that, if certain specified events occur (e.g. a fixed-term contract being brought to a premature end by the employer), the employer will pay the employee an agreed sum in satisfaction of any claims that he or she may have. Such clauses are called 'liquidated damages clauses' or 'pay in lieu of notice' (PILON) clauses. It should be noted that it is unlikely that a court or tribunal will find that there is a genuine bilateral agreement terminating the contract, though there are restricted circumstances in which it may do so.

Dismissal with notice

Termination occurs when either party informs the other clearly and unequivocally that the contract is to end, or the circumstances are such that it is clear that termination was intended or that it can be inferred that termination was intended. The words used to terminate the contract must be capable of being interpreted as words of termination. The principles are the same whether the termination consists of dismissal by the employer or resignation by the employee.

In the case of dismissal by the employer, phrases such as 'I hereby give you notice of dismissal' are clear. Problems arise, however, where there is a row between the employer and the employee and words are used in the heat of the moment. If the words used by the employer are not ambiguous or could be interpreted only as amounting to words of dismissal, then the conclusion is clear. If, on the other hand, the words used are ambiguous and it is not clear whether they do amount to words of dismissal (e.g. 'You're finished with me'), it is necessary to look at all the circumstances of the case, particularly the intention with which the words were spoken, and consider how a reasonable employee would, in all the circumstances, have understood them.

In *Rai* v. *Somerfield Stores Ltd* (2004), the EAT said that a notice which enables an employer to terminate an employee's contract of employment only if the employee does or does not perform a particular act specified in the notice, which only the employee can choose whether or not to perform, is not an unequivocal notice to terminate the employment. In the case in question the employee was told that if he did not return to work by a specified date his contract would be regarded as terminated. The EAT said that this did not amount to dismissal with notice.

Dismissal without notice

Dismissal without notice – usually called 'summary dismissal' – is on the face of it a breach of contract, since the employee has been denied his or her contractual entitlement to termination of the contract by notice or to the expiry of a fixed-term contract. The employer's defence in such a case is that the employee has committed a repudiation of the contract sufficiently serious to justify dismissal without notice. In effect, therefore, the issue in a summary dismissal case is not whether the employee was dismissed but whether the dismissal was in breach of contract and thus 'wrongful'.

RESIGNATION

The requirements in the case of resignation by an employee are very similar to those for dismissal. It is important for employers to know whether an employee has resigned, since if they treat the employee as having resigned when that is not in fact the case, they may be held to have dismissed the employee. If the employee's resignation is prompted by a repudiatory act or breach of contract by the employer, that may be treated as constructive dismissal by the employer.

An example of this situation is the case of *Evening Standard Co. Ltd* v. *Henderson* (1987). The employee was employed as the production manager of the *Standard*. His contract required one year's notice of termination and provided that, while it lasted, he was not to engage in work outside the company without special permission. He was offered a similar position with a competitor newspaper and gave his employers two months' notice of termination. The employers sought an injunction to restrain him from undertaking employment with or providing assistance to any competitor of theirs in breach of his contract of employment. The Court of Appeal said that there was no serious issue as to liability, since the employee's contract would continue until the expiration of the one-year notice period, unless his employers accepted his repudiation. If, during that time, he were to work for the competitor, he would be in breach of contract. The court went on to hold that the balance of convenience favoured the granting of an injunction.

Constructive dismissal

Different considerations arise where the employee's resignation is prompted by a breach of contract or a repudiatory act committed by the employer. In that case the resignation will be called a 'constructive dismissal'. It should be noted that this term has no statutory authority and is merely a convenient shorthand expression for resignation on the part of the employee prompted by an action on the part of the employer which may be categorised as a repudiatory act or a breach of contract. In *Western Excavating (ECC) Ltd* v. *Sharp* (1978), at p. 226, Lord Denning MR said:

> If the employer is guilty of conduct which is a significant breach going to the root of the contract of employment, or which shows that the employer no longer intends to be bound by one or more of the essential terms of contract, then the employee is entitled to treat himself as discharged from any further performance ... (T)he conduct must ... be sufficiently serious to entitle him to leave at once ...

In this case the applicant was suspended without pay by the employer as a disciplinary sanction following his taking time off work without permission. Owing to the severe financial difficulties this placed the applicant in, he then asked his employer for his accrued holiday pay, and when this was refused he asked for a loan, which was also refused. He then resigned, and pursued a claim for constructive dismissal based on unreasonable conduct on the part of the employer.

The decision in *Omilaju* v. *Waltham Forest London Borough Council* (2005) sought to clarify the concept of constructive dismissal, and in particular the idea of 'last straw' offences. In this case, Omilaju was an employee of the council, who during a thirty-month period had issued five separate sets of proceedings in the employment tribunal against the employer council. The case arose when the council refused to pay the employee's full salary when he was absent attending one of these hearings, which was in accordance with the council policy requiring employees to apply for unpaid or annual leave to attend tribunal hearings. As a result the employee resigned, and claimed in his resignation letter that there had been a breach of his trust and confidence in the employer, that this was 'the last straw in a series of less favourable treatments that I have been subjected to over a period of years'. Along with other claims brought before the employment tribunal on these events, the tribunal dismissed his claim for constructive dismissal. On appeal the Employment Appeal Tribunal considered the concept and nature of a 'last straw' offence, and whether this would be sufficient.

The EAT held that a final straw, not itself a breach of contract, could result in a breach of the implied term of trust and confidence. In order for this to suffice the act had to be part of a series of acts which when considered cumulatively amounted to a breach of the implied term. The nature of the final act itself need not be 'unreasonable' or 'blameworthy' conduct, nor need it be a significant breach. So long as the act in question contributed something to the breach, and was indeed the final act of a series of acts, constructive dismissal might have taken place. The EAT held that the test to be applied in determining whether an act was capable of breaching the implied term was an objective one, and accordingly found that the conduct of the council in this case was not capable of contributing to a breach of the implied term of trust and confidence.

WRONGFUL DISMISSAL

A contract of employment is terminable by notice, express or implied, unless the contract is for a fixed term or for the completion of a specific task or contains an exhaustive enumeration of the grounds upon which it may be terminated. If, therefore either party terminates the contract summarily, i.e. without notice, the other party has the right at common law to sue for breach of contract. If the defendant's summary termination of the contract was a response to an action on the part of the plaintiff, a defence may be available. But he or she must be able to show that the plaintiff's behaviour amounted to a breach of a serious term of the contract or a repudiation of the contract which entitled him or her to terminate the contract summarily. The plaintiff's breach need not have been known at the time of the summary dismissal (see *Boston Deep Sea Fishing & Ice Co.* v. *Ansell* (1888)).

If the summary dismissal by the employer is not justified, the employee will be treated as having been wrongfully dismissed; if the employer's conduct causes the employee to resign and that conduct is held to be repudiatory or in breach of contract, the employee's contract will be treated as having been breached. An action for wrongful dismissal or breach of contract is heard in the county court or High Court; the employment tribunals also now have jurisdiction in such cases where damages are claimed.

An example is *Bliss* v. *South East Thames Regional Health Authority* (1987), where the employers acted in a way which the Court of Appeal held to be a repudiation of the employee's contract, by requiring him to submit to a medical examination and suspending him when he refused. They held that the employer's action was in breach of contract by requiring the employee, without reasonable cause, to submit to the medical examination and, when he refused, by suspending him. That was a breach of the implied term that they would not without reasonable cause conduct themselves in a manner likely to impair or destroy the relationship of trust and confidence between employer and employee. The breach was so serious as to go to the root of the contract and to entitle the employee to treat the contract as at an end. The breach was a continuing breach until the employers lifted the suspension. After the employers withdrew the requirement and lifted the suspension, they offered to give him time to make up his mind about his future intentions and to pay him while he did so. They then tried to argue that his acceptance of his salary affirmed the contract so as to preclude him from accepting their repudiation, as he purported to do. The Court of Appeal held that he had not affirmed the contract by his conduct in accepting the salary payments and he was entitled to accept the repudiation. The court took the view that the cardinal factor was that the employer was prepared to give the employee time to make up his mind and to pay him while he was doing so. *Dietmann* v. *London Borough of Brent* (1988) (CA), the employee's acceptance of the offer of employment was held to amount to acceptance of the employer's repudiation so as to preclude her from injunctive relief.

INTERACTIVE LEARNING

1   Consider the differences between *wrongful, unfair* and *constructive* dismissal.
2   Brian is a principal surveyor in Mancaster Council. He earns £70,000 p.a. He has just been given his notice by the council's chief executive. His line manager has informed him that he must clear his desk immediately. The reason for the notice is that he has been criticised in a local newspaper for his recent plan for pedestrian walkways in the town centre. Advise Brian.

8

Dismissal

The right to claim unfair dismissal was created by the Industrial Relations Act 1971. Despite the numerous changes in the legislative provisions brought about by the changes of political fashion, the basic structure of the provisions remains similar to what was originally enacted. There have, of course, been numerous additions, but the structure enacted by the 1971 Act is still discernible.

Potential claimants must fulfil certain requirements before being able to make a complaint of unfair dismissal. These are:

1 They must be an employee.
2 They must have been 'continuously employed' for one year.
3 They should not be in one of the excluded classes.
4 They must present their complaint of unfair dismissal within three months of the 'effective date of termination'.
5 They must have been 'dismissed'.

QUALIFICATIONS

The Employment Rights Act (ERA), s. 94(1) provides that an employee has the right not to be unfairly dismissed by his or her employer. This right is made subject to other provisions of the ERA, such as the provision excluding those who have reached 'normal retiring age' or who are over sixty-five: see s. 109(1). Thus the right not to be unfairly dismissed extends only to employees; it is not available to those who are self-employed. The distinction between employees and self-employed persons was examined in Chapter 2.

Excluded categories

The following categories of employee are excluded from the legislation:

1 employees employed under illegal contracts;
2 those covered by diplomatic or State immunity;
3 employees of international organisations;
4 Crown employees;
5 parliamentary staff;
6 employees over retirement age;
7 short-term and casual employees;
8 employees affected by national security;
9 share fishermen;
10 those in the police service and members of the armed forces.

Continuity of employment

Continuity of employment is important in the present context because the statutory rights are available only to employees who have been 'continuously employed' for the requisite period of time. In the case of the unfair dismissal rights, that period is one year: see ERA, s. 108(1) (as amended). Continuity of employment is also used to compute the amount of a redundancy payment and of a basic award of compensation for unfair dismissal.

The date at which the employee must have the minimum period of employment is the 'effective date of termination', defined by ERA, s. 97, as either the date when the notice given to the employee expires or, in the case of a summary dismissal, the date of the summary dismissal. The starting date for the calculation is the day on which he or she started work: ERA s. 211(1). That means the day on which the employment under the contract began, not the day on which the employee started to perform the duties.

DISMISSAL

In the case of unfair dismissal complaints, ERA, s. 95, contains the definition of dismissal; the statutory provision is exhaustive. The combined effect of the statutory provisions and judicial interpretations of them is that some situations clearly fall within them, for example, an actual dismissal; some situations are deemed to be a dismissal, for example, a resignation prompted by a repudiatory breach on the employer's part or the expiry of a fixed-term contract. Some situations (for example, a frustrating event or a voluntary resignation unprompted by action on the employer's part) are outside the definition.

It is important when determining whether an action falls within the definition of dismissal to start with the statutory language and then to examine the relevant judicial decisions. This is different from the common law position involving wrongful dismissal, to which the statutory definition does not apply. It is also important to bear in mind that an event which is treated as dismissal by the statute may not be dismissal at common law. For example, the expiry of a limited-term contract is expressly treated as dismissal by ERA, s. 95(2)(b). At common law, however, it will not amount to dismissal.

The basic statutory definition of dismissal in ERA, s. 95(1), is as follows:

an employee is dismissed by his employer if (and ... only if) –

(a) the contract under which he is employed is terminated by the employer (whether with or without notice),
(b) he is employed under a contract for a limited term and that term expires without being renewed under the same contract, or
(c) the employee terminates the contract under which he is employed (with or without notice) in circumstances such that he is entitled to terminate it without notice by reason of the employer's conduct.

The statutory definition set out above is the basic definition used in both the unfair dismissal and (with a slight difference of wording) the redundancy payments provisions in the ERA 1996. The third type of dismissal in the definition is usually called 'constructive dismissal', but that is not a term to be found in the legislation. For a discussion of the first and third concepts – actual and 'constructive' dismissals – reference should be made to Chapter 7, where they are examined.

Reason for dismissal

Once it has been established that the employee has been dismissed, an unfair dismissal claim will fall to be decided in two stages. The first stage consists of establishing what was the reason for the dismissal; at the second stage the tribunal must be satisfied that the employer acted reasonably in dismissing for the given reason.

The 'potentially fair' reasons are so called because they can potentially justify dismissal, but they do not necessarily justify dismissal, since ERA,

s. 98(4), obliges the tribunal to decide whether the employer acted reasonably or unreasonably in treating the reasons as sufficient for dismissing the employee. In a complaint of unfair dismissal involving the potentially fair reasons, ERA, s. 98(1), places the burden on the employer to show the reason (or, if there was more than one, the principal reason) for the dismissal. He or she must then show that the reason falls within one of the five specific categories set out in ss. 98(2) and (1)(b).

As part of the process of establishing the reason for the dismissal ERA, s. 92, entitles an employee to be given a written statement of reasons for the dismissal by the employer. This right is considered first, after which the 'potentially fair' reasons will be considered.

As stated above, ERA, s. 92, entitles an employee to a written statement of reasons for the dismissal by the employer. This right is limited to the extent that it does not apply where the dismissal was constructive (s. 92(1)), and requires the employee to have served at least one year's continuous service. The statement must 'be of such a kind that the employee, or anyone to whom he may wish to show it, can know from reading the document itself why the employee has been dismissed' and must 'contain a simple statement of the essential reasons for the dismissal'. Where such a statement is unreasonably refused, the claimant may complain to an employment tribunal, which may consequently declare what it believes to be the true reasoning behind the dismissal and also has the power to award a sum equal to two weeks' pay.

In a complaint of unfair dismissal involving the so-called 'potentially fair' reasons, ERA, s. 98(1), places the burden on the employer not only to show the reason (or, if there was more than one, the principal reason) for the dismissal but also to show that the reason falls within one of the five categories set out in ss. 98(2) and (1)(b), which are:

1 capability or qualifications;
2 employee's conduct;
3 redundancy;
4 statutory requirements;
5 'some other substantial reason'.

The House of Lords' decision in W. *Devis & Sons Ltd* v. *Atkins* [1977] (applied by the EAT in *Vauxhall Motors Ltd* v. *Ghafoor* (1993) established the principle that an employer may not bring in evidence of what happened after the dismissal or of events which occurred before the dismissal but which did not come to his or her knowledge until afterwards. In such a case, the consequence is likely to be a decision that the employee was unfairly dismissed, but the evidence of the misconduct will be relevant to the question of remedies.

Capability

ERA, s. 98(3), defines 'capability' as 'capability assessed by reference to skill, aptitude, health or any other physical or mental quality', and 'qualifications' means 'any degree, diploma or other academic, technical or professional qualification relevant to the position which the employee held'. In *Shook* v. *Ealing London Borough Council* (1986) the EAT stressed that under ERA, s. 98(2)(a), the reason for dismissal must relate to the employee's capacity and to the performance of his or her duties under the contract of employment. It is not necessary to show that the employee's incapacity (in this case disabilities caused by back trouble) would have affected the performance of all that he or she might be required to do under the contract.

Misconduct

There is no statutory definition of 'conduct'. Apart from the overlap between conduct and capability, conduct itself has been held to embrace a wide range of actions. Its scope includes gross misconduct, such as theft, violence, negligence and working in competition with the employer, and lesser matters, such as clocking offences or swearing. What may be called 'off-duty' conduct will fall within this head, if it in some way bears upon the relationship between the employer and the employee, particularly where criminal offences are involved. Such cases should be thoroughly investigated (see *British Home Stores Ltd* v. *Burchell* (1980)).

Some other substantial reason

The fifth category of reason is stated in ERA, s. 98(1)(b), to be 'some other substantial reason of a kind such as to justify the dismissal of an employee holding the position which the employee held'. This is a fairly wide category of reasons. The most common examples relate to the business needs of the employer and have tended to involve a refusal by the employee to agree to a change in contractual terms or a refusal to agree to a reorganisation falling short of redundancy (see *RS Components* v. *Irwin* (1973) and *Hollister* v. *National Farmers' Union* (1979)).

PROCEDURES

Once a potentially fair reason under the ERA has been established, it is then necessary to consider whether the employer acted fairly in dismissing for that reason. S. 98(4) states as follows:

> the determination of the question whether the dismissal is fair or unfair (having regard to the reason shown by the employer –
>
> (a) depends on whether in the circumstances (including the size and administrative resources of the employer's undertaking) the employer acted reasonably or unreasonably in treating it as a sufficient reason for dismissing the employee, and
> (b) shall be determined in accordance with equity and the substantial merits of the case.

The effect of s. 98(4) is that there is no burden of proof on either the employer or the employee. It is therefore wrong for an employment tribunal to place the burden on the employer of satisfying it that he or she acted reasonably (see *Post Office (Counters) Ltd* v. *Heavey* (1990); *Boys' and Girls' Welfare Society* v. *McDonald* (1996); and *Hackney London Borough Council* v. *Usher* (1997)).

The Court of Appeal has stressed that appeals to the EAT and beyond lie only on points of law and has discouraged attempts to dress up questions of fact as questions of law. But it is clear that the question of fairness cannot be considered solely as one of fact, and therefore unappealable. It is best described as a mixed question of fact and law. The tenor of the Court of Appeal decisions is to restrict considerably the circumstances in which appeals may be made to the EAT from employment tribunals' decisions and to discourage the EAT from reversing the tribunals' decisions because it would have reached a different conclusion.

This approach may be characterised as the 'reasonable decision' approach. It was summarised by Browne-Wilkinson J (as he then was) in *Iceland Frozen Foods Ltd* v. *Jones* (1983).

> The correct approach ... is as follows:
>
> (1) the starting point should always be the words of s. (98(4)) themselves;
> (2) in applying the section an employment tribunal must consider the reasonableness of the employer's conduct, not simply whether they (the members of the employment tribunal) consider the dismissal to be fair;
> (3) in judging the reasonableness of the employer's conduct an employment tribunal must not substitute its decision as to what was the right course to adopt for that of the employer;
> (4) in many, though not all, cases there is a band of reasonable responses to the employee's conduct within which one employer might take one view, another quite reasonably take another;

(5)   the function of the employment tribunal, as an industrial jury, is to determine whether in the particular circumstances of each case the decision to dismiss the employee fell within the band of reasonable responses which a reasonable employer might have adopted. If the dismissal falls within the band the dismissal is fair: if the dismissal falls outside the band, it is unfair.

In *Foley* v. *Post Office* (2000), Mummery LJ robustly endorsed the *Iceland Frozen Foods* approach saying that the decision itself, which had been approved and applied by the Court of Appeal, 'remains binding on this court, as well as on the employment tribunals and the Employment Appeal Tribunal'. He described the disapproval by the EAT of that approach as 'an unwarranted departure from authority'.

As the case law has developed over the years, adherence to the notion of procedural fairness has gained ground and considerable importance has been attached to it. It means that dismissal may be made unfair by the use of an unfair procedure (e.g. lack of warnings or opportunity for the employee to state his or her side of the case), even where the reason is a perfectly good one. This was stressed by the House of Lords in its decision in *Polkey* v. *AE Dayton Services Ltd* (1988), which has a particularly important bearing on the whole area of procedural fairness. The case involved the question whether a dismissal which would be unfair because of failure to follow a fair procedure can be held to be fair if the employer is able to establish that following a fair procedure would have made no difference to the outcome. The House of Lords said that the correct question is whether the employer has been reasonable or unreasonable in deciding that the reason for dismissing the employee was a sufficient reason, not whether the employee would nevertheless have been dismissed even if there had been prior consultation or warning. Whether the employer could reasonably have concluded that consultation or warning would be useless so that the failure to consult or warn would not necessarily render the dismissal unfair was a matter for the employment tribunal to consider in the light of the circumstances known to the employer at the time of the decision to dismiss.

In *Polkey* the employee was made redundant following a reorganisation of the business. The employee claimed unfair dismissal on the basis that he had not been warned or consulted about his redundancy. The employers pleaded the no-difference rule, arguing that even if they had warned and consulted, Polkey would have been made redundant anyway. A tribunal accepted the reasoning forwarded by the employer, finding the decision to dismiss was fair.

However, the House of Lords overruled the no-difference rule, and held that a reasonable employer would have warned and consulted whether the redundancy was inevitable or not, and by failing to do so the employer had acted unreasonably. The dismissal was therefore found to be unfair. The emphasis on procedural fairness, which is highlighted by this case, should not be allowed to distract the commentator from observing that it is as much about compensation as about procedural fairness. Effectively, the House of Lords is drawing attention to the fact that the observance of procedure is important but that, if the tribunal's judgment is that the outcome would have been a fair dismissal even had a fair procedure been observed, the issue becomes one of correctly reflecting that judgment in the measure of compensation.

This reflection makes one wonder whether the introduction of ERA, s. 98A(2), by the EA 2002, s. 34(2), which was supposed to reverse the effect of the decision in *Polkey*, actually makes any difference. This new provision states that the failure by an employer to follow a procedure in relation to the dismissal of an employee 'shall not be regarded for the purposes of s. 98(4) as by itself making the employer's action unreasonable if he shows that he would have decided to dismiss the employee if he had decided to follow the procedure'.

The statutory procedures

S. 34(1) of the 2002 Act has introduced a new provision into the ERA, s. 98A(1), which links the new procedures enacted in the 2002 Act with the unfair dismissal provisions. It comes into play where one of the procedures set out in EA 2002 Sch. 2, Part 1 (relating to dismissal and disciplinary procedures) applies. In that case, an employee is to be treated as unfairly dismissed if the procedure has not been completed and the non-completion is 'wholly or mainly attributable to failure by the employer to comply with its requirements'. Part 1 sets out two alternative dismissal and disciplinary procedures, the 'standard' procedure and the 'modified' procedure. The latter applies in cases of alleged misconduct.

These provisions came into force on 1 October 2004.

The statutory dismissal and disciplinary procedures (SDP) apply principally to employees although the Secretary of State has the power to extend the scope of the provision to other workers if she thinks fit, and apply it to dismissal as well as to disciplinary action short of dismissal (such as suspension). There are common features in both procedures that must also be adhered to, in addition to the procedures themselves:

1   Each step and action under the procedure must be taken without unreasonable delay.
2   Both the timing and location of the meetings must be reasonable.
3   Meetings must be conducted in a manner that enables both employer and employee to explain their cases.
4   In the case of appeal meetings which are not the first meeting the employer should so far as is reasonably practicable be represented by a more senior manager than attended the first meeting (unless the most senior manager attended that meeting).

The 'standard' procedure

1   The employee must be informed in writing of the reasons why the employer is contemplating dismissing or taking disciplinary action against him or her, and should be invited to a meeting to discuss the matter further.
2   No action should be taken prior to the meeting, except where the disciplinary action taken is suspension. The employee must take all reasonable steps to attend.
3   Following the meeting the employee must be informed of the employer's decision, and made aware of any appeal procedures available in the result that they are unsatisfied by the outcome.
4   In the event of an appeal, the employee must inform the employer of their intention to do so. Consequently the employer must invite the employee to attend a further meeting, which the employee must take all reasonable steps to attend.
5   The disciplinary action or dismissal can take place before the appeal meeting.
6   After the appeal, the employer must inform the employee of his final decision.

The 'modified' procedure (relating only to alleged misconduct)

1   The employer must set out in writing the employee's alleged misconduct which has led to the dismissal and the employee's right to appeal against dismissal, and send a copy of the statement to the employee.
2   In the event of a desire to appeal the employee must inform the employer.

3 If the employee opts to appeal then the employer must invite the employee to a further meeting, which the employee must take all reasonable steps to attend.
4 Following the appeal the employer must inform the employee of his or her final decision.

Also brought in by the Employment Act 2002 are statutory grievance procedures, once more consisting of a 'standard' and a 'modified' procedure. The standard (SGP) procedure mirrors that found in the SDP, except for the first stage, where in this case it is for the employee to write a letter notifying the employer of his or her grievance, as opposed to the employer writing to inform the employee of reasons for the discipline or potential dismissal.

The 'modified' statutory grievance procedure again is used only in certain circumstances, and is to be utilised when the person raising the grievance is a former employee, and is as follows:

1 The employee must inform the employer in writing of his or her grievance,
2 The employer must set out his or her response in writing and send it to the former employee.

AUTOMATICALLY UNFAIR DISMISSAL

The following types of dismissal will be treated as automatically unfair:

1 dismissals in connection with trade union membership and activities, or trade union recognition;
2 dismissal for participation in official industrial action;
3 dismissal of an employee in connection with leave for family reasons, including paternity and adoption leave;
4 dismissal for reasons connected with health and safety;
5 dismissal of a shop or betting worker for refusing Sunday work;
6 dismissal in connection with an employee's rights under the Working Time Regulations;
7 dismissal for reasons relating to an employee's performance of his or her duties as an occupational pension fund trustee;
8 dismissal for reasons relating to an employee's performance of his or her duties as an employee representative;
9 dismissal for making a 'protected disclosure';
10 dismissal for assertion of a statutory right;

11   dismissal of an employee in connection with the national minimum wage legislation;

12   dismissal in connection with an employee's rights under the Tax Credits Act 1999;

13   dismissals of employees arising under paragraph 28 of the Transnational Information and Consultation of Employees Regulations 1999;

14   dismissals arising under regulation 7 of the Part-time Workers (Prevention of Less Favourable Treatment) Regulations 2000;

15   dismissals arising under regulation 6 of the Fixed-term Employees (Prevention of Less Favourable Treatment) Regulations 2002;

16   dismissal of a worker in connection with the statutory right to be accompanied at a disciplinary or grievance hearing.

REMEDIES

The remedies available to an employee whose complaint of unfair dismissal succeeds are a re-employment order or compensation.

Reinstatement and re-engagement orders

The main remedies for unfair dismissal were intended to be reinstatement and re-engagement orders, and the whole tenor of the statutory provision is to suggest that the employment tribunal should apply those remedies first: see ss. 112–16. In reality, though, few re-employment orders are made.

A reinstatement order is an order to the employer to treat the applicant as if he or she had not been dismissed. In deciding whether to make an order, the tribunal must comply with the requirements of s. 116(1), and take into account the following factors: the complainant's wishes; the practicability for the employer of compliance with the order; and, where the complainant caused or contributed to some extent to the dismissal, whether it would be just to order reinstatement.

If the tribunal decides not to order reinstatement, it should then consider whether to order re-engagement: s. 116(2). A re-engagement order is an order that the employee should be engaged by the employer, or by a successor of the employer or an associated employer, in employment comparable to that from which he or she was dismissed, or 'other suitable employment': s. 115(1). In deciding whether to make the order, the tribunal must have regard to the requirements of s. 116(3). The three factors it must take into account are similar to those mentioned above in relation to reinstatement orders. In relation to the second factor (practicability), however, the tribunal must consider the practicability of re-engagement with a successor of the employer or an associated employer.

The effect of an order of reinstatement is to give the employee his or her old job back; it will include an ancillary order for arrears of pay between the date of dismissal and the date of reinstatement. There is no statutory maximum to the amount which may be ordered to be paid under s. 114(2)(a). The effect of a re-engagement order will be to give the employee a job similar to the one from which he or she was dismissed. S. 115(2) requires the tribunal when making the order to specify the terms of re-engagement, again including arrears of pay.

If the employer does not comply fully with the terms of a reinstatement or re-engagement order, the tribunal must award such an amount of compensation as it thinks fit having regard to the loss sustained by the employee, subject to the maximum permissible: s. 117(1) and (2). If the employer totally fails to comply, then the tribunal must go on to award compensation in the usual way and it must also make an additional award of compensation in accordance with s. 117(3)(b).

Compensation

An employment tribunal will award compensation if it makes no order for re-employment, or if it makes such an order but the employer totally fails to comply with it. Compensation may consist of the following elements: a basic award; a compensatory award; and an additional award.

If the employment tribunal makes a finding of unfair dismissal, it must first consider whether to make an order for the re-employment of the applicant. If he or she does not wish such an order to be made or if the tribunal decides against making an order, it will proceed to award compensation. If it does make an order, but the employer totally fails to comply with it, the tribunal will make an additional award and then go on to award compensation in the usual way. In most cases, compensation usually consists of a basic award and a compensatory award.

The *basic award* is calculated in the same way as a redundancy payment. It is necessary to take the complainant's age, length of continuous employment on the effective date of termination and the amount of gross weekly pay. Reductions in the basic award may be made where the employee is near retirement, where the employee unreasonably refuses an offer of reinstatement, where the employee's conduct before dismissal makes it just and equitable to make a reduction, where the employee has already received a redundancy payment, and where the employee has received an *ex gratia* payment from the employer.

The *compensatory award* should be 'such amount as the tribunal considers just and equitable in all the circumstances having regard to the loss sustained by the complainant in consequence of the dismissal in so far as that loss is attributable to action taken by the employer': see s. 123(1). The maximum amount of compensatory award that may be awarded is currently £58,400 as from 1 February 2006. The heads of loss which the compensatory award may cover were set out in *Norton Tool Co. Ltd* v. *Tewson* (1972) and are: (1) immediate loss of wages; (2) manner of dismissal; (3) future loss of wages; and (4) loss of protection in respect of unfair dismissal or dismissal by reason of redundancy. A fifth head of loss was subsequently added: loss of pension rights.

It is important to note that in two types of unfair dismissal the amount of the compensatory awards is unlimited. These are cases in which the dismissal is automatically unfair because it was a health and safety case and covered by s. 100 or because the employee made a 'protected disclosure' and the dismissal fell within s. 103A, or because the employee was selected for reasons falling within either of those provisions. This is an exception to the general rule that the compensatory award is subject to a limit, the current limit, as mentioned being of £58,400.

INTERACTIVE LEARNING

1   List the remedies available for unfair dismissal.
2   Arnold, Bruce and Clive work for Kings Ltd, which is in financial difficulty. A cheque for £1,000 has been fraudulently cashed by an employee of the company, and Mr Phipps, the managing director, believes the employee to have been Arnold. When confronted by Mr Phipps, Arnold denies the offence, but Mr Phipps is convinced that only Arnold would have been in a position to do such a thing and dismisses him without consulting the other directors. Bruce, who is a senior foreman and has worked at the company's headquarters all his eight years of employment, has been told that he will be moved to a small factory some ten miles distant. When Bruce refuses to move, he too is dismissed. Clive is told that in order to effect economies the company will not be giving him the annual pay rise to which he is contractually entitled. Clive remonstrates and two days later hands in his notice. Advise Kings Ltd of any liabilities and/or remedies they may have in relation to Arnold, Bruce and Clive.

9

Redundancy and Business Transfers

The statutory provisions relating to redundancy payments originated in the Redundancy Payments Act 1965. Employees are generally entitled to the right not to be unfairly dismissed, as has been seen, only if they have been continuously employed for one year (Employment Rights Act (ERA) 1996, s. 108(1)).

In general, an employee dismissed for redundancy will be advised to complain of unfair dismissal or to make a dual claim. This is because a complaint under the unfair dismissal provisions enables the Employment Tribunal to decide whether the employer's decision to dismiss was reasonable in all the circumstances, whereas the redundancy payments provisions merely enable the tribunal to decide whether the statutory presumption of redundancy has or has not been rebutted. Further, the unfair dismissal provisions give an employee the possibility of receiving greater compensation, in the form of the basic award, which is calculated in the same way as a redundancy payment, *plus* a compensatory award, which is not available under the redundancy payments provisions. In the case of a dual claim, the successful employee will receive either a basic award or a redundancy payment, but not both, since ERA, s. 122(4), contains set-off provisions.

REDUNDANCY

Redundancy is defined in s. 139(1) as follows:

> [A]n employee who is dismissed shall be taken to be dismissed by reason of redundancy if the dismissal is wholly or mainly attributable to –

(a) the fact that his employer has ceased or intends to cease

   (i)   to carry on the business for the purposes of which the employee was employed by him, or
   (ii) to carry on that business in the place where the employee was so employed, or

(b) the fact that the requirements of that business

   (i)   for employees to carry out work of a particular kind, or
   (ii) for employees to carry out work of a particular kind in the place where the employee was employed by the employer,

have ceased or diminished or are expected to cease or diminish.'

The definition of redundancy in s. 139(1) uses the phrase 'in the place where the employee was ... employed'. In earlier cases the issue was regarded as being determined by reference to the employee's contract, in other words whether the employer had contractual authority, express or implied, to order the employee to move; or, to put it another way, what degree of contractual mobility the employee was subject to (see *Nelson* v. *BBC* (1977)). The effect was that if the employee was required to move to another factory within the radius of the mobility obligation because of the closure of the factory where he or she worked, it would not be possible to claim a redundancy payment, since there had not been a cessation of the business in the place where he or she was employed.

In *Bass Leisure Ltd* v. *Thomas* (1994), on the other hand, what has been called the 'factual' test was used. There, the EAT said that 'the place' where an employee is employed does not extend to any place where the employee may be contractually required to work; the question is primarily a factual one and the only relevant contractual terms are those which define the place of employment and its extent.

The next question is what amounts to a dismissal by reason of redundancy. The authorities were reviewed by the EAT in *Safeway Stores plc* v. *Burrell* (1997), which contains a valuable analysis of the approaches propounded by the courts in recent years. The employee's dismissal arose from a reorganisation or 'delayering' of the employers' management structure, with the result that there were fewer management positions than before, which gave rise to redundancies. The tribunal decided that he had not been dismissed by reason of redundancy, since the work done by the employee still had to be done and, therefore, the requirements of the employers' business for employees to carry out work of a particular kind had not ceased or diminished. The EAT reversed this decision and said that he had been dismissed by reason of redundancy. It said that a three-stage process is involved in determining whether a dismissal for redundancy has taken place:

1   Was the employee dismissed?
2   Had the requirements of the employer's business for employees to carry out work of a particular kind ceased or diminished? If so
3   Was the dismissal of the employee caused wholly or mainly by the state of affairs identified in stage 2?

It said that, at stage 2, the only question to be asked is whether there is a cessation or diminution in the employer's requirements for employees (not the applicant) to carry out work of a particular kind and that, at this stage, it is irrelevant to consider the terms of the employee's contract. At stage 3 the tribunal is concerned with causation. This decision is important and should prompt a re-evaluation of the meaning of dismissal for redundancy. It is also notable for its emphasis on the words of the statute.

The *Safeways* decision was approved by the House of Lords in *Murray* v. *Foyle Meats Ltd* (1997) Lord Irvine said:

> The language of [s. 139(1)(b)] ... asks two questions of fact. The first is whether one or other of various states of economic affairs exists. In this case, the relevant one is whether the requirements of the business for employees to carry out work of a particular kind have diminished. The second question is whether the dismissal is attributable, wholly or mainly, to that state of affairs. This is a question of causation ... The key word in the statute is 'attributable' and there is no reason in law why the dismissal of an employee should not be attributable to a diminution in the employer's needs for employees irrespective of the terms of his contract or the function which he performed.

In *Murray* v. *Foyle Meats Ltd* the employees worked as meat plant operatives. Although they normally worked in the slaughter hall, they could, under their contracts of employment, be required to work elsewhere in the plant, and on occasion they did. Falling business led to fewer employees being needed in the slaughter hall, and consequently the applicants were made redundant. The applicants argued that the selection pool was too narrow, on the basis that they were also required to work elsewhere under their contracts. They claimed that their dismissals were unfair.

The House of Lords held that the requirements of the employer for employees to work in the slaughter hall had diminished and that this was the reason that the applicants were redundant. The pool for selection was therefore correct, and the dismissal was fair by way of redundancy. Lord Irvine, however, commented:

> Both the contract test and the function test miss the point. The key word in the statute is 'attributable' and there is no reason in law why the dismissal of an employee should not be attributable to a diminution in the employer's needs for employees irrespective of the terms of his contract or the function he performed.

Offer of alternative employment

S. 138 deals with the situation where an employee who is under notice of redundancy (or who has been constructively dismissed) is offered alternative employment. As will be seen from the discussion below, there are circumstances in which an employee will be treated as not having been dismissed. In such circumstances, there will be no entitlement to a redundancy payment, simply because entitlement to a payment depends upon having been dismissed for redundancy and, therefore, if there is no dismissal, there can be no entitlement. Once, however, the employee is found to have been dismissed, he or she may be disentitled from receiving the payment which would otherwise be payable if there is held to have been an unreasonable refusal of a suitable offer: see ss. 141 and 146.

S. 138 deals with the situation where an employee who is under notice of redundancy (or who has been constructively dismissed) is offered alternative employment. The point of its provisions, which follow on from the basic definition of dismissal in s. 136 (which is very similar to the definition of dismissal in s. 95 in relation to the unfair dismissal provisions), is to determine in what circumstances the employee is to be treated as having been dismissed.

S. 138 caters for two alternative possibilities: either that the terms and conditions of the new employment are the same as those of the old, or that they are different. In both cases, there must be an offer of renewal of the contract or of re-engagement under a new contract; an offer of re-engagement must be made before the ending of the employment under the previous contract. The renewal or re-engagement must take effect immediately on the ending of the previous employment, or within four weeks. If any of the conditions are not complied with, there will be a dismissal. Where the new contract is the same as the old, and all the conditions of s. 138(1) are complied with, there will be no dismissal and s. 213(2) will preserve continuity of employment. In *SI (Systems & Instruments) Ltd* v. *Grist and Riley* (1983), the EAT said that, on a proper construction of what is now s. 138(1), a distinction is to be drawn between cases of renewal and re-engagement. In cases of renewal, the offer need not be made before the termination of the contract of employment, but in cases of re-engagement under a new contract, the offer must be made before termination. 'Renewal' includes 'extension': ERA, s. 235(1).

Redundancy payment

The calculation of a redundancy payment is based on the following factors:

1   the employee's age at the relevant date (in most cases, the same date as the effective date of termination in unfair dismissal cases;
2   the number of years of continuous employment;
3   the amount of gross weekly pay.

The calculation is subject to the following limits:

1   the number of years used in the calculation may not exceed 20: s. 162(3);
2   the amount of a week's pay may not exceed a figure set annually by the Secretary of State, the amount being currently £290: s. 227(1), as amended by the Employment Rights (Increase of Limits) Order 2005 (SI 2003/3038).

Redundancy payments are calculated in accordance with ERA, s. 162, and the total amount arrived at may be subject to a deduction in certain cases, mainly in the case of misconduct or where employees are near retirement age. Social security benefits paid to the employee are not deductible. The method of calculation is to take each year of continuous employment, working backwards from the relevant date. For each year of continuous employment the amount of the redundancy payment is assessed on the basis of the employee's age at the beginning of the year. For each year in which the employee was aged forty-one or more (but not more than sixty-four), one and a half week's pay is payable; for each year in which he or she was between twenty-two and forty-one, one weeks' pay; for each year over the age of eighteen between the time he or she started work and twenty-two, half a week's pay: ss. 162(2) and 211 (2). Thus an employee employed for twenty-years and made redundant at sixty-two will receive a redundancy payment reckoned on the basis of the years of continuous employment from sixty-two going back to forty-two. The current maximum redundancy payment that can be awarded at present is £8,400. Employment before the age of eighteen may not be counted: s. 211(2). The employee's period of continuous employment will be treated as starting on his or her eighteenth birthday if that date is later than the starting date.

BUSINESS TRANSFERS

The provisions of Directive 2001/23/EC (which, as already seen, derive from the 1977 directive) have now been considered in a considerable number of decisions in the European Court of Justice (ECJ). In *Foreningen af Arbejdsledere i Danmark* v. *Daddy's Dance Hall A/S* (1988), one of the cases of lasting significance in this area, the Court said:

> [T]he objective of Directive 77/187 is to ensure as far as possible the safeguarding of employees' rights in the event of a change of proprietor of the undertaking and to allow them to remain in the service of the new proprietor on the same condition as those agreed with the vendor. The Directive therefore applies as soon as there is a change, resulting from a conventional sale or a merger, of the natural or legal person responsible for operating the undertaking who, consequently, enters into obligations as an employer towards employees working in the undertaking, and it is of no importance to know whether the ownership of the undertaking has been transferred.

Article 1(1)(a) of the directive states that it is to apply to 'any transfer of an undertaking, business or part of an undertaking or business to another employer as a result of a legal transfer or merger.' Article 1(1) goes on to state:

> (b) there is a transfer within the meaning of this Directive where there is a transfer of an economic entity which retains its identity, meaning an organised grouping of resources which has the objective of pursuing an economic activity, whether or not that activity is central or ancillary.

These new provisions were substituted for Council Directive 98/50/EC and are intended to clarify the legal concept of transfer in light of the previous case law of the ECJ.

Article 3 provides for the automatic transfer to the transferee of the transferor's rights and obligations arising from a contract of employment or from an employment relationship existing on the date of the transfer. In *Katsikas* v. *Konstantinidis* (1993) the European Court of Justice held that this provision does not preclude an employee employed by the transferor from objecting to the transfer to the transferee of the contract of employment or employment relationship. It said that in such cases it is for the Member States to decide what the fate of the contract of employment or employment relationship with the transferor should be.

Article 4(1) (as substituted) states:

> The transfer of the undertaking, business or part of the undertaking or business shall not in itself constitute grounds for dismissal by the transferor or the transferee. This provision shall not stand in the way of dismissals that may take place for economic, technical or organisational reasons entailing changes in the work force.

Article 4(2) goes on to provide that if the contract of employment or the employment relationship is terminated because the transfer involves a substantial change in working conditions to the detriment of the employee, the employer is to be regarded as having been responsible for the termination. The relationship between Article 3(1) as interpreted in the *Katsikas* case (above) and Article 4(2) was considered by the ECJ in *Merckx and Neuhuys* v. *Ford Motor Co. Belgium SA* (1997). The distinction made by the Court is between the employee of his or her own accord deciding not to continue with the employment relationship with the transferee, in which case the *Katsikas* case will apply, and terminating the contract because the transfer involves a substantial change in working conditions, such as a change in the level of remuneration; in the latter case, Article 4(2) will apply. Much will depend upon the facts of any given case.

Relevant transfer

The starting point for a consideration of this question is *Spijkers* v. *Gebroeders Benedik Abattoir* (1986). In that case, the ECJ emphasised that the aim of the directive is to ensure 'the continuity of employment relationships existing within a business, irrespective of a change of owner' and said that the decisive criterion is 'whether the business in question retains its identity'. It went on to say:

[I]t is necessary to consider all the facts characterising the transaction in question, including the type of undertaking or business, whether or not the business's tangible assets, such as buildings and movable property are transferred, the value of its intangible assets at the time of the transfer, whether or not the majority of its employees are taken over by the new employer, whether or not its customers are transferred and the degree of similarity between the activities carried on before and after the transfer and the period, if any, for which those activities were suspended. It should be noted, however, that all those circumstances are merely single factors in the overall assessment which must be made and cannot, therefore, be considered in isolation.

In *Süzen* v. *Zehnacker Gebdudereinigung GmbH Krankenhausservice, Lefarth GmbH (Party joined)* (1997) the question was whether the termination of a cleaning contract with one contractor and the grant of the contract to another contractor amounted to a transfer within the directive. As in the *Merckx* case, there was no transfer of tangible or intangible assets. The Court reiterated what it had said in previous cases, that the decisive question is whether the entity in question retains its identity. It said that, although the absence of a contractual link between the transferor and the transferee or (as here) the two undertakings successively granted the cleaning contract might point to the absence of a transfer, it was not conclusive. It added the transfer may take place in two stages, through the intermediary of a third party such as the owner or the person putting up the capital, and stressed that the transfer must relate to a stable economic entity whose activity is not limited to performing one specific works contract. The ECJ ruled:

The term entity thus refers to an organised grouping of persons and assets facilitating the exercise of an economic activity which pursues a specific objective ... [T]he mere fact that the service provided by the old and the new awardees of a contract is similar does not therefore support the conclusion that an economic entity has been transferred. An entity cannot be reduced to the activity entrusted to it. Its identity also emerges from other factors, such as its work force, its management staff, the way in which its work is organised, its operating methods or indeed, where appropriate, the operational resource available to it ... The mere loss of a service contract to a competitor cannot therefore by itself indicate the existence of a transfer ... In those circumstances, the service undertaking previously entrusted with the contract does not, on losing a customer, thereby cease fully to exist, and a business or part of a business belonging to it cannot be considered to have been transferred to the new awardee of the contract.

In the *Süzen* case Mrs Süzen was a cleaner who worked for a company which had a contract to clean a school. When this contract came to an end, the contract was awarded to another company, and Süzen along with seven of her colleagues was dismissed. She sought a declaration that her contract had been transferred to the new contractor. The ECJ followed the reasoning above to find that Süzen's contract had not been transferred. The Court further stated that the directive applies only where there is a transfer of significant tangible or intangible assets, or a transfer of a significant proportion of the work force who provided the service prior to the transfer.

The ECJ in *Oy Liikenne AB* v. *Liskojärvi and Juntunen* (2001) was faced with similar questions to those raised in the *Süzen* case. The facts of the case were that the operation of seven bus routes was awarded to Oy Liikenne AB; they had previously been operated by Hakunilan Liikenne Oy. Hakunilan dismissed forty-five drivers, of whom thirty-three were re-engaged by Oy Liikenne; no vehicles or other assets connected with the operation of the bus routes were transferred, although Oy Liikenne bought uniforms from Hakunilan for some of the drivers who entered its service. The applicants were among the thirty-three drivers who were taken on by Oy Liikenne. They claimed that there had been a transfer of an undertaking and that they were entitled to enjoy the more favourable terms and conditions applied by their previous employer. In such a situation Directive 77/187 might not apply in the absence of a transfer of significant tangible assets from the old to the new contractor.

The European Court of Justice in *Abler* v. *Sodexho MM Catering GmbH* (2004) once more considered the question of what is a 'transfer' for the purposes of the directive. Abler suggests that the correct approach in determining this concept is first to place the business in its correct sectoral context, before evaluating all the relevant circumstances in discovering whether a transfer of a stable economic entity has taken place.

The facts of the case were that Abler worked as a kitchen help at an Austrian hospital. The contractor by which she was employed lost the catering contract, which was awarded to a different contractor. Consequently Abler, along with other hospital catering staff, was made redundant. Abler contended that a transfer of undertaking had taken place. The new contractor argued that no transfer had occurred on the basis that it had refused to take on any of its predecessor's employees, there was no contractual relationship existing between the two contractor firms, and that all they had done was taken over hospital premises and equipment formerly used by the previous contractors. The case was referred to the ECJ, the question being whether there could be a transfer of part of a business within the meaning of Article 1 of the directive where a hospital catering undertaker used substantial parts of the tangible assets formerly used by its predecessor but had expressly refused to take on its predecessor's employees.

The ECJ held the sector in which the business operated was an important consideration. In an equipment-based sector, such as catering in the current case, failure to take on an essential part of the staff previously employed by the former contractor did not preclude the existence of a transfer of an economic entity which maintained its identity within the meaning of the directive. Catering could not be viewed as an activity based essentially on manpower, since a significant amount of equipment was required. The transfer of the premises and equipment necessary for the preparation and distribution of meals was sufficient to make this a transfer of an economic entity. The Court considered it irrelevant that the assets that were taken over as a result of the 'transfer' were not owned by the former contractor. This approach suggests that the decisive criterion in such cases is whether the tangible assets 'contribute significantly' to the activity and does not seem to take into account the possibility that there may be factors pointing to the conclusion that the entity retains its identity.

Dismissal

Article 4(1) contains two propositions. The first is that a transfer of an undertaking 'shall not in itself constitute grounds for dismissal ...' The second is that the previous statement 'shall not stand in the way of dismissals that may take place for economic, technical or organisational reasons entailing changes in the work force'.

TUPE REGULATIONS 1981

The effect of the TUPE regulations 1981 is that they afford protection to employees where there is a 'relevant transfer' of an 'undertaking'. Where there is a relevant transfer, an employee's contract will be automatically transferred to the person to whom the undertaking is transferred. The importance of the decisions of the ECJ considered above lies in the fact that courts and tribunals in the United Kingdom are required to interpret the regulations so that, as far as possible, they conform to the directive.

The definition of 'undertaking' is to be found in regulation 1(1): ' "undertaking" includes any trade or business'. Recent decisions in the Court of Appeal and the EAT have drawn heavily on the case law of the ECJ when considering whether a particular entity amounts to an undertaking. In *Whitewater Leisure Management Ltd* v. *Barnes* (2000) the EAT said that there are two formulations which can be used to identify whether there is an economic entity. The first asks whether there is 'a stable and discrete economic entity'; the alternative version asks whether the entity is 'sufficiently structured and autonomous'. The EAT suggested that the expression 'distinct cost centre' might be helpful. Had the EAT considered the ECJ decision in *Allen* v. *Amalgamated Construction Co. Ltd* (2000), it might have reached a different conclusion. That case said that there may be a transfer of an economic entity even where there is no transfer of the plant and equipment necessary to carry out the activity because they are supplied by the person granting the contract.

'Relevant transfer'

A 'relevant transfer' is defined in regulation 3(1) as 'a transfer from one person to another of an undertaking situated immediately before the transfer in the United Kingdom or a part of one which is so situated'. Regulation 3(2) applies the regulations to transfers by sale or other disposition or by operation of law, but transfers of share capital (e.g. as in take-overs) and dispositions of physical assets are excluded. Regulation 3(4) provides that a transfer may be effected by a series of two or more transactions and that it may take place whether or not any property is transferred to the transferee by the transferor. Very shortly after the decision in *Süzen*, the Court of Appeal heard the appeal from the High Court in *Betts* v. *Brintel Helicopters Ltd* (1997). The case involved the loss by one company (Brintel) of a contract to provide helicopter services and its transfer to another (KLM). KLM took over only rights associated with the contract and engaged none of Brintel's employees. The main issue in the Court of Appeal was whether there was a transfer of an undertaking, in other words whether the undertaking had retained its identity in the hands of the transferee.

This decision may be contrasted with the decision of another division of the Court of Appeal, about a year later, in *ECM (Vehicle Delivery Service) Ltd* v. *Cox* (1999). A contract to distribute cars ('the VAG contract') was lost by one contractor and awarded to ECM. They chose to organise the contracted service in a different way; they dispensed with the previous contractor's base and refused to engage any of the staff employed on the vehicle delivery contract because they had asserted that their employment was protected by TUPE. The Court of Appeal upheld the decision of the tribunal and the EAT that there had been a relevant transfer. The argument of ECM in the Court of Appeal was that there was no transfer of an undertaking, although it accepted that there was an undertaking carried on by the previous contractor. The basis of their argument was that *Süzen* signalled a change of emphasis in the ECJ and that the position on transfers of undertakings following that decision was that, where the only continuing feature is the nature of the activity itself and all that continues is the service itself, it is impossible to find that an undertaking has been transferred. So in the case in question, it was argued, all that continued was the activity of delivering cars under the VAG contract. Mummery LJ, with whom the other lords justices agreed, rejected that argument and held that the employment tribunal had applied the correct test, as laid down in *Spijkers* and subsequent cases. He also observed that the tribunal was entitled to have regard, as a relevant circumstance, to the reason why the employees were not taken on by ECM. He suggested that the importance of *Süzen* had been overstated and pointed out that the ECJ had not overruled its previous interpretative rulings. He also observed that the criteria laid down by the ECJ still involve consideration of 'all the facts characterising the transaction in question' as identified in *Spijkers*.

On the completion of the relevant transfer, regulation 5(2) provides that all the transferor's (i.e. old employer's) rights, powers, duties and liabilities 'under or in connection with' the employee's contract of employment are transferred and anything done before the transfer is completed by the transferor in relation to the contract is treated as done by the transferee. The wording of this regulation suggests that, when a relevant transfer takes place, liability passes to the transferee and the transferor drops out of the picture. It should be noted, however, that a transfer under regulation 5 will be effective irrespective of whether the employees knew of the transfer and the identity of the transferee.

In *Secretary of State for Employment* v. *Spence* (1986), the Court of Appeal held that regulation 5 was concerned with contracts of employment subsisting at the moment when the undertaking was transferred. As the employees' contracts were not subsisting at the moment of transfer, they had been dismissed before the relevant transfer. This question was subsequently considered by the House of Lords, in *Litster* v. *Forth Dry Dock & Engineering Co. Ltd (in receivership)* (1989). The House of Lords held that the regulations should be given a purposive construction in a manner which would accord with the decisions of the European Court of Justice on the directive and, where necessary, words should be implied to achieve that effect. There should be implied into regulation 5(3) after the words 'immediately before the transfer' the words 'or would have been so employed if he had not been unfairly dismissed in the circumstances described by regulation 8(1)'. In reaching this decision, the House of Lords followed the decision of the ECJ in *P. Bork International A/S* v. *Foreningen af Arbejdsledere i Danmark* (1989) and *Marleasing* v. *LA Comercial* (1992).

Dismissal – regulation 8

Dismissals on the transfer of an undertaking are governed by regulation 8. Regulation 8(1) sets out the general rule, that an employee dismissed either before or after a relevant transfer will be treated as automatically unfairly dismissed, if the transfer or a reason connected with it is the reason or principal reason for the dismissal. The rule applies to employees both of the transferor and of the transferee. The general rule does not apply, however, when there is an 'economic, technical or organisational reason entailing changes in the work force for either the transferor or transferee either before or after a relevant transfer' and that is the reason or principal reason for dismissing the employee: reg. 8(2). In that case, the reason will be treated as 'some other substantial reason' within ERA, s. 98(1)(b), and the fairness of the reason must then be considered by the tribunal under s. 98(4). The correct approach is to consider, first, whether regulation 8(1) applies so as to make the dismissals automatically unfair; if it does not, then the tribunal should consider whether regulation 8(2) applies.

One issue which has now been resolved by the House of Lords concerned the effect of a dismissal which is brought about by the transfer of an undertaking. In *Wilson* v. *St Helens Borough Council* (1998) and *Meade* v. *British Fuels Ltd* (1998) two groups of dismissals were involved. The group involved in the *Wilson* case were dismissals for an economic or technical reason and thus within regulation 8(2); the group involved in the *Meade* case were dismissals for a reason connected with the transfer and thus within regulation 8(1). Lord Slynn of Hadley gave the main speech. It centred round the issue whether a dismissal of an employee brought about by a transfer of an undertaking is or is not a nullity. He took the view that the provisions of regulation 8(1) and (2) point to a dismissal being effective and not a nullity and do not create an automatic obligation on the part of the transferee to continue to employ employees who have been dismissed by the transferor. He then went on to consider whether TUPE complies with the directive. Having considered the relevant case law of the ECJ, he concluded that the directive did not create a Community law right to continue in employment which does not exist in national law and that TUPE gives effect to and is consistent with the directive. Thus, if an employee is dismissed by the transferor and re-engaged by the transferee, the latter will assume any liability for dismissals incurred by the transferor. The employee will not be able to insist on the observance by the transferee of his or her previous terms or conditions and will be bound by the terms and conditions agreed with the transferee. The dismissal will thus be unfair by virtue of regulation 8(1) but not ineffective.

Amending TUPE 1981

The amended Acquired Rights Directive (ARD) of 1998 will bring about important changes in the current regime.

First, although the definition of a 'transfer of undertaking' has not changed, Article 1 has expanded the concept in the view of offering more guidance as to when TUPE applies. The amendments regarding the expanded definition reflect the existing case law:

1   The concept of an 'economic entity' has been adopted, with the ARD referring to the 'transfer of an economic entity which retains its identity, meaning an organised grouping of resources which has the objective of pursuing an economic activity, whether or not that activity is central or ancillary'.
2   It has been made clear that the ARD applies to both public and private businesses, regardless of economic aims.

3 Administrative reorganisation of public administrative authorities' or the transfer of administrative functions between public administrative authorities has been expressly excluded from the scope of the directive.

Other amendments involve the position of occupational pension rights, information and consultation, and insolvency:

1 Although previously excluded, the amended ARD allows Member States to allow the transfer of occupational pension schemes or survivor's benefits.
2 Representatives of affected employees must now be informed of the date or proposed date of the transfer. Where no representatives exist, the employees must be informed of:

    (a) the date or proposed date of the transfer;
    (b) the reason for the transfer;
    (c) the legal, economic and social implications of the transfer;
    (d) any measures envisaged in relation to the employee.

Previously employees themselves were limited to only receiving information on the date of the transfer.

3 The amended ARD allows Member States to relax the laws as regards applying the ARD in the context of insolvencies. Furthermore, Member States are now able to provide that in relation to all transfers during insolvency proceedings which are under the supervision of a competent public authority:

    (a) the transferee is not liable for the transferor's debts arising from the contracts or the employment relationship which were payable before the transfer;
    (b) there may be a variation of terms and conditions through agreement with the employee representatives if this is designed to safeguard employee positions by allowing the business to continue.

The transferor must be in 'a situation of serious economic crisis, as defined by national law' in order to negotiate such amendments.

The government has been extremely busy in reforming TUPE, undertaking a consultation paper and subsequently releasing draft regulations. The consultation paper concentrated on the following areas:

1 Transfers within public administration. This was aimed at removing the uncertainty that was present with regard to transfers in the public sector.
2 Service provision changes. The question was posed as to whether any changes were required as regards service provision (for example, contracting out).
3 Occupational pensions. How should these be dealt with?
4 How the regulations should apply in insolvency situations.
5 How to deal with the transfer of employee liability information.

As a result of this consultation paper the government produced a set of draft regulations. These draft regulations suggest the following amendments will be made:

1 The definition of a TUPE transfer will be broadened. This will take a similar position to that stated in the case law, and will make express inclusion of contracting-out transfers.
2 Comparable pensions will be protected and transferred.
3 'Seagoing' vessels will finally come within the scope of the regulations.

The revised TUPE regulations 2006 are expected to come into force on 6 April 2006.

INTERACTIVE LEARNING

1 Consider what impact the revised 2006 TUPE regulations will have.
2 Bryony's manager, Phil, has informed her that her job as marketing analyst is no longer required. However, she has just heard that Phil's son, Peter, has been offered a new job as forecast and new ventures manager. Bryony has been given a month's pay. (She earns £5,000 p.a., is twenty-six years of age and has been with the company four years.) Advise Bryony of her rights in this scenario.
3 'The European Court of Justice continues the tide of confusion in relation to business transfers.' Discuss this statement illustrating your answer with case law examples.

10

Health and Safety

Health and safety in the workplace are very important. The requirement of compulsory employer's liability insurance since 1969 ensures such safety. However, although UK health and safety law has been long established under the 1974 Health and Safety at Work, etc., Act (HASAWA), it is now influenced more by EU law. Also, what is unique about this area of employment law is that its interaction with both civil and criminal law (in that an employer can be sued for injuries and can be prosecuted) allows an interesting legal enforcement of these important obligations.

In order to understand the full picture of health and safety protection afforded to employees this chapter considers: the common law position; the statutory regime; and the influence of Europe in the regulation of safety in the workplace.

HEALTH AND SAFETY AT COMMON LAW

Claims at common law as regards health and safety matters generally take one of three forms:

1 breach by the employer of the implied term that the employee's place of work is reasonably safe for the performance of the employment duties;
2 breach of a statutory duty;
3 negligence.

The implied duty to ensure that the working environment is reasonably safe

All UK employers are under a duty to have regard to the safety of their employees. Furthermore, specific statutory duties are owed by UK employers to the following:

1 employees;
2 members of the public;
3 visitors (namely contractors and other employees working on the employer's premises).

Safety at work is so important that under the Employment Rights Act 1996 employees are protected from dismissal or victimisation by the employer in health and safety cases, unjustified refusal to deal with a safety grievance.

Employers are therefore obliged to see that the place where their employees work is reasonably safe in all the circumstances. A system of work includes:

1 the method;
2 staffing of operations;
3 provision of equipment;
4 supervision.

The provisions contained in HASAWA seek to complement rather than supersede the common law provision relating to safety.

The duty to provide a safe system of work is not an absolute one. The duty is to take reasonable steps to provide a system which will be reasonably safe, having regard to the dangers necessarily inherent in the operation. In deciding what is reasonable the courts examine:

1 the size of the danger;
2 the likelihood of an accident occurring;
3 the consequences of the occurrence of an accident;
4 the steps needed to eliminate all risk and the cost of doing so (*Edwards* v. *National Coal Board* (1949)).

An employer is under a duty to take reasonable care to see that his employees are not subjected to any unnecessary risk of injury. Where a risk is not obvious, the employee will succeed only if he or she can show that the state of knowledge in the relevant industry at the relevant time was such that the employer knew or ought to have known of the risk. But an employer must keep reasonably abreast of developing knowledge, and if he has greater than average knowledge of the risks he may have to take greater than average precautions.

Breach of a statutory duty

This type of claim is the less frequently invoked. In order to make a claim for breach of a statutory duty, the onus is on the employee to prove the following:

1   A statute in this area exists.
2   The claimant is covered by the statutory duty.
3   The duty is placed on the defendant. This is usually expressly dealt with by the regulations in question.
4   The defendant has acted in breach of the duty imposed. This is not as easy to prove as it sounds, the courts not giving clear guidance on the precise standard of care that is required.
5   The harm suffered fell within the scope of the statute, and was of the nature that the statute was designed to protect against.
6   The harm was a result of this breach.

Common law action for the tort of negligence

For an action of negligence to succeed, the following must be proved:

1   The employer owed the employee a duty of care.
2   There has been a breach of that duty by the employer.
3   The employee suffered damage as a result of that breach.

The duty of care
The classic definition of a duty of care owed in the employment context was formulated by Lord Wright in *Wilsons & Clyde Coal Co. v. English* (1938), finding that the duty was threefold: (1) 'provision

of a competent staff of men'; (2) 'adequate material'; (3) 'proper system
and effective supervision'. But what does the concept of a duty of care
cover today? The duty of care owed by the employer to the employee
today can be summarised thus:

1 *Duty to provide a competent staff of men.* This duty concerns finding suitable and competent fellow employees, and to provide adequate and relevant training where appropriate.
2 *Duty to provide adequate and safe equipment.* This duty, unlike the
   others, is one of strict liability, governed by the Employers' Liability
   (Defective Equipment) Act 1969. In effect, where the employee is
   injured in the course of employment, the injury was caused by
   equipment provided by the employer, and the defect is the fault
   (wholly or partly) of a third party, then the injury will be regarded
   as being caused by the negligence of the employer.
3 *Duty to provide a safe system of work.* This duty covers the provision of a safe workplace, safe methods of carrying out the work, as
   well as the supervision of the work. (See above for a full discussion
   on this implied term.)
4 *Duty to protect the employee from psychiatric injury at work.* An
   employer may also be liable in certain circumstances for psychiatric
   illness caused by work if it was reasonably foreseeable (see *Walker* v.
   Northumberland County Council (1995). In order to recover compensation for psychiatric injury, it is necessary for the conditions set
   out in *Alcock* v. *Chief Constable of South Yorkshire Police* (1992)
   to be satisfied:

   (a) there must be a close tie of love and affection between the
       claimant and the victim;
   (b) the claimant must have been present at the accident or its
       immediate aftermath;
   (c) the psychiatric injury must have been caused by direct percep-
       tion of the accident or its immediate aftermath and not by
       hearing about it from someone else.

Breach of the duty owed

Once it has been established that the employer owes the employee a
duty of care, then one must consider whether this duty has been
breached by the employer's negligence. In determining this, the courts

must consider the personal relationship between the employer and the employee claiming the breach, and therefore is subjective in nature. As a result of this approach, where an employee is deemed inexperienced, or where the consequences of such a breach are significantly increased through the personal circumstances of the employee, the standard of care owed is found to be higher: see *Paris* v. *Stepney Borough Council* (1951).

Causation

The final element, which at times proves the most difficult to satisfy, is that of causation. The employee has to show that the injury in question was in fact caused by the negligence being complained of. Difficulties in this area tend to arise when an employee is claiming a stress-related illness as being caused by the employer's negligence. However, the courts appear to have eased the burden in *Smith* v. *Leech Brain & Co. Ltd* (1962), establishing a rule that appears somewhat to aid the employee in showing causation. In this case an employee suffered a personal injury as a result of his employers' negligence. Owing to the nature of the work involved, some injury was clearly foreseeable. However, it was not foreseeable that the employee would develop cancer from the injury that was suffered. The tribunal held the employers to be liable. Since the employers could have foreseen the initial injury suffered, they were liable for all the consequences that were born of that injury.

Contributory negligence

Where the employee's negligence has in some way added to the injury caused by the employer's initial negligence, the damages awarded may be reduced accordingly. The Law Reform (Contributory Negligence) Act 1945, s. 1(1), states that damages 'shall be reduced to such extent as the court thinks just and equitable having regard to the claimant's share in the responsibility for the damage'.

Consent

Where an employee has consented to the damages caused through negligence, he generally loses the right to a claim for negligence. This covers the situation where an employee accepts and runs the risk accordingly. Two elements must be present to claim this as a defence:

1 The employee had knowledge of the risk.
2 The employee of his own accord voluntarily accepted the risk.

Vicarious liability

As well as owing a duty of care directly to an employee, an employer may also be liable for negligent acts by a third party. This is known as vicarious liability. The extent of such liability differs, depending on who the third party is, and therefore we must consider the different categories of persons this may involve, the employees and independent contractors.

Employees

An employer is liable for the acts of his employee if they are committed in the course of the employee's employment. In order to establish that the employer is vicariously liable for the acts of an employee, two things must be shown: the person who was guilty of the negligent act was an employee; the act committed must be one for which the employer was responsible.

Independent contractors

Generally, an employer is not liable for the acts of an independent contractor engaged by him, provided that he exercised due diligence in selecting the contractor for the task. Except for the common law duty of an employer to provide his employees with a safe place of work, as an occupier of premises he owes his employees, and other visitors, the common duty of care imposed by the Occupiers' Liability Act 1957. The extent of the duty which is owed to trespassers is defined by the Occupiers' Liability Act 1984. That is, an occupier of premises may be the owner or the licensee (i.e. a person who merely has permission to occupy by the owner). An occupier need not have exclusive control over premises in order to have a duty to persons who visit those premises; more than one person may owe a duty in respect of the same premises.

The extent of the duty of care is defined in OLA 1957, s. 2(2) as:

> a duty to take such care as in all the circumstances of the case is reasonable to see that the visitor is reasonably safe in using the premises for the purposes for which he is invited or permitted by the occupier to be there.

In defining the extent of the duty, the courts will take into account the *degree of control over the premises actually enjoyed* by the occupier and, if applicable, the division of duties between the multiple occupiers of the same premises. For example, if an employer leases a warehouse to store his products and an employee of that company suffers an accident due to the state of repair of the warehouse, the assessment of liability will depend on the actual degree of control exercised by the warehouse owner and the employer.

Under OLA 1957 s. 2(2), the duty to ensure that the visitor is reasonably safe in using the premises for the purpose for which he or she is there does not extend to dangers occurring to employees of contractors as a result of activities they are performing on the premises. The House of Lords, in its landmark ruling in *Fairchild* v. *Glenhaven Funeral Services Ltd* (2002), HL, allowed claimants to recover damages from their former employers in relation to mesothelioma, resulting from the negligent exposure to asbestos.

The cases under appeal in the *Fairchild* case concerned employees who contracted mesothelioma as a result of exposure to asbestos dust during the course of employment. Medical opinion suggested that at least 90 per cent of mesothelioma cases were caused by such exposure.

The House of Lords, relaxing the causal test of negligence in special cases such as those involved here, stated that:

> The conventional test of causation in claims for damages for negligence, that a claimant must prove that, but for the defendant's wrongful conduct, he would not have sustained the harm in question, can be departed from in special circumstances where justice so requires. A lesser degree of causal connection was justified in the circumstances of these cases, where the claimant was employed at different times and for different periods for more than one employer, each subject to a duty to protect the claimant against a known risk of contracting mesothelioma from the inhalation of asbestos dust ... it was sufficient that the breach of duty materially increased the risk of the claimant contracting the disease. Although this meant that an employer may be held liable for damage which he had not caused, that was preferable to the claimant being unable to recover damages because, in the present state of medical knowledge, the doctors are unable to say which employer's breach of duty caused the disease.

Unanimously, their Lordships held that the victim, on grounds of so-called 'justice', should not be deprived of a remedy because it cannot be established which of a series of different employers caused the alleged harm. As Lord Nicholls put it: 'Any other outcome would be deeply offensive to instinctive notions of what justice requires and fairness demands.' Consequently, employers may now be held liable for damage which they did not cause. The House of Lords established a right to damages by departing from the orthodox test of causation where justice so requires, by establishing a notion of joint liability. For instance, on the facts of this case, it was sufficient that the employers' breach of duty materially increased the risk that the claimants would contract mesothelioma. Therefore, the *Fairchild* ruling presupposes negligence by all employers. Clearly, the impact of this historic ruling is that once a breach of duty can be established, then each employer becomes liable for the full damages. This ruling makes no reference to the application of the principle of apportionment of damages in such circumstances.

Faulty work by contractors

If an accident occurs as a result of faulty work by an independent contractor employed at the premises which the employer occupies, OLA 1957, s. 2(4)(b), provides that:

> the occupier is not to be treated without more ('without more' in the sense of 'on those facts alone') as answerable for the danger if in all the circumstances he had acted reasonably in entrusting the work to an independent contractor and had taken such steps (if any) as he reasonably ought in order to satisfy himself that the contractor was competent and that the work had been properly done.

Thus, if injury is caused to a visitor to the premises by the fault of an independent contractor, the occupier will not be held liable for the injury or damage so caused if he can show that:

1　He acted reasonably in entrusting the work to the independent contractor. (It may be held to be reasonable to employ an independent contractor where the work to be done is of a skilled or specialist nature and is beyond the capacity of the employer.)
2　He exercised a reasonable degree of care in selecting the independent contractor to see that he was competent to do the task entrusted to him.
3　He checked so far as was possible to see that the work was properly carried out.

THE STATUTORY REGIME: THE HEALTH AND SAFETY AT WORK, ETC., ACT 1974

Duties of employers

The Health and Safety at Work, etc., Act 1974 ('HASAWA' as it is more commonly termed) sets out the guiding principles to be adhered to by employers governing health and safety in the workplace. It also establishes the Health and Safety Executive (HSE), granting powers to inspectors to issue improvement and prohibition notices (www.hse.gov.uk).

The principles contained in HASAWA 1974 seek to:

1   secure the health, safety and welfare of persons at work;
2   protect persons other than persons at work against risks to health or safety arising out of, or in connection with, the activities of persons at work;
3   control the keeping and use of explosive or highly flammable or otherwise dangerous substances, and generally prevent the unlawful acquisition, possession and use of such substances.

Regulations and codes of practice issued under HASAWA 1974 give effect to the general principles set out and also to enforce the provisions of the legislation. This power to produce regulations has been utilised on a number of occasions. Among the more important regulations made under HASAWA 1974 are the:

1   Health and Safety (First-Aid) Regulations 1981.
2   Reporting of Injuries, Diseases and Dangerous Occurrences Regulations 1995.
3   Electricity at Work Regulations 1989.
4   Control of Substances Hazardous to Health Regulations 2002.

All UK employers are obliged to:

1   prepare a written safety statement;
2   organise and make arrangements for carrying out that policy;
3   inform (giving notice to) all their employees.

Since July 2000 employers are required to use a revised version of the poster; additional detail is provided on aspects of the Management of

Health and Safety at Work Regulations 1999 and new sections have been incorporated for the insertion of the names and locations of safety representatives and competent persons together with their health and safety responsibilities.

Employers who carry on undertakings in which for the time being they employ fewer than *five* employees are exempted from the requirement of s. 2(3) by the Employers' Health and Safety Policy Statements (Exception) Regulations 1975.

Employers and self-employed people are obliged to conduct their undertakings, so far as is reasonably practicable, in a way which will ensure that persons who may be affected, not being their employees, are not exposed to risks to health or safety (HASAWA 1974, s. 3(1), (2)). The conduct of the undertaking extends to the manner in which equipment is made available for use by employees outside business hours.

In *R* v. *Associated Octel Co. Ltd* (1997) the House of Lords held that an employer was criminally liable under s. 3(1) for the negligence of an independent contractor in respect of injuries sustained by an employee of the contractor while undertaking maintenance and repair work for the employer. The conduct of the employer's undertaking could cover ancillary activities carried out by independent contractors, particularly when the activity was carried out on the employer's premises.

In the case the defendants operated a large chemical plant, which was labelled by the HSE as a 'major hazard site'. The company, on an annual basis, shut the plant down for maintenance and repair. The 1990 shutdown necessitated the repair of the lining of a tank within the chlorine plant, with the contract being awarded to a firm of specialist contractors who had a history of regular past dealings with the company. During the time carrying out the repairs, the contractor's eight employees were employed virtually full-time on the defendant's site. One of the employees, Mr Cuthbert, was assigned the task of cleaning out the tank. Whilst undertaking this task, the bulb of the light he was using broke, and ignited the bucket of highly inflammable acetone which was being used for the cleaning. This in turn caused a flash fire and an explosion, and Mr Cuthbert as a result was badly burned.

The House of Lords on these facts held that the defendants were guilty of a criminal offence under s. 3 of the HASAWA 1974. The repair work undertaken was considered to fall within the scope of the employer's duty under s. 3(1) 'to conduct his undertaking in such a way as to ensure, so far as is reasonably practicable, that persons not in his employment who may be affected thereby are not thereby exposed to risks to their health and safety'. In determining this, Lord Hoffman stated the question to be asked was 'whether the activity in question can be described as part of the employer's undertaking.' It was clear on these facts that the work was carried out under the control of the defendants, and was a part of the employer's undertaking.

Regulations may be introduced compelling employers and self-employed people to give information relating to health and safety to people (not being their employees) who may be affected by the way in which they conduct their undertakings (HASAWA 1974, s. 3(3)).

Duties of employees

Every employee while at work has the duty:

1 to take reasonable care for the health and safety of himself and of other persons who may be affected by his acts or omissions at work;
2 to co-operate with his employer, or any other person, in ensuring that requirements or duties imposed by the relevant statutory provisions (including those specified in Sch. 1) are complied with.

(HASAWA 1974, s. 7.)

ENFORCEMENT

Under HASAWA 1974, s. 10, the HSE is given the task of safety enforcer.

Inspectors

The HSE is responsible for the enforcement of the Health and Safety at Work, etc., Act 1974. Pursuant to the Health and Safety (Enforcing Authority) Regulations 1998, the enforcement powers under HASAWA 1974 cover all the 'relevant statutory provisions', which comprise its provisions. Since 2002 the HSE has operated under its newly revised enforcement policy statement setting out its specific criteria to enable its inspectors to decide when to investigate health and safety incidents, and to prosecute for breaches.

Every inspector has the power to:

1   enter premises;
2   take measurements and photographs and make other records;
3   take samples of articles or substances found on any premises;
4   dismantle or subject to any process or test any dangerous substance;
5   destroy the dangerous or potentially dangerous substance or article;
6   take possession of a dangerous or potentially dangerous article or substance to examine it, to ensure that it is not tampered with or to ensure that it is available for use as evidence in any proceedings.

An inspector may require persons to answer questions in the course of his investigations and to sign a declaration of the truth of their answers. He may require the production of books and documents and take copies of them. If he requires any facilities or assistance in the course of his investigations, he may require the person able to do so to provide him with such facilities.

Improvement notices

If an inspector is of the opinion that a person:

1   is contravening one or more of the relevant statutory provisions; or
2   has contravened one or more of those provisions in circumstances that make it likely that the contravention will continue or be repeated, he may serve on that person a notice (referred to as 'an improvement notice').

An improvement notice must:

1   state that he is of that opinion;
2   specify the provisions which in his opinion are being or have been contravened;
3   give particulars of the reasons for his opinion;
4   require that person to remedy the contravention within a specified period.

Prohibition notices

If an inspector regards any activities as involving or potentially involving *a risk of serious personal injury*, he may serve on the person in control of those activities a notice known as 'a prohibition notice' (HASAWA 1974, s. 22).

A prohibition notice must:

1 state the opinion of the inspector;
2 specify the matters which in his opinion give or, as the case may be, will give rise to the risks;
3 where in his opinion any of those matters involves or will involve a contravention of any of the relevant statutory provisions, state that he is of that opinion, specify the relevant provision or provisions, and give particulars of the reasons why he is of that opinion;
4 direct that the activities to which the notice relates shall not be carried on by or under the control of the person on whom the notice is served unless the matters specified in the notice and any associated contraventions so specified have been remedied.

Defence

Many of the statutory provisions contain the modification 'so far as is reasonably practicable', or 'practicable' or to use 'the best practicable means to do something'. In those cases the onus is on the accused to prove that it was not practicable or not reasonably practicable to do more than was in fact done to satisfy the duty or requirement, or that there was no better practicable means than was in fact used to satisfy the duty or requirement (HASAWA 1974, s. 40). However, where proceedings are brought under HASAWA 1974, s. 33(1)(g) for contravention of an improvement notice, the offence is established if there has been non-compliance with a requirement of the notice irrespective of whether compliance was reasonably practicable.

EU LEGISLATION

The European Union has significant influence in the area of health and safety. A plethora of EU-wide health and safety laws has emerged under the auspices of the Framework Directive, in force in the United Kingdom since 1993. For instance, seven so-called 'daughter' directives, laying down detailed requirements, were initially adopted under this directive:

1 minimum requirements for safety and health in the workplace;
2 use of machines and equipment;
3 use of personal protective equipment;
4 use of visual display units;
5 handling of heavy loads;
6 working time;
7 Protection of Young People at Work.

Further directives have been adopted on carcinogens, biological agents, construction sites, health and safety signs, and the protection of pregnant workers.

INTERACTIVE LEARNING

1 How has Europe impacted upon health and safety law in the UK?
2 Louise is employed by Stokeshire Football Club as a secretary to the managing director. On a winter's morning she drives to work. After a busy day in the office she returns to the car park, where she slips and breaks her leg. The car park has a notice which reads: 'Owners park at their own risk.' Advise Stokeshire FC on any liabilities (if any) which might arise from this accident.
3 Devise a safety policy, ensuring compliance with any safety legal obligations.

11

Employment Tribunals

The annual report of the Employment Tribunals service (the ETS Report) reported that in the year 2004–05 there were approximately 165,072 applications to Employment Tribunals.

COMPOSITION OF EMPLOYMENT TRIBUNALS

The primary legislation governing employment tribunals (ETs) is the Employment Tribunals Act 1996 (ETA), although their constitution and rules of procedure are contained in the Employment Tribunals (Constitution and Rules of Procedure) Regulations 2004. Employment Tribunals consist of a three-member panel, i.e. a legally qualified chairperson and two lay members (sometimes called 'wing members') who are not legally qualified. The chairperson, who is appointed by the Lord Chancellor as either full-time or part-time, must be a barrister or solicitor of at least seven years' standing, while the lay members (who are all part-time) are chosen after consulting organisations representing employees and those representing employers. This means that the lay members have experience of each side of industry, i.e. management and employees, and together provide what is sometimes called an 'industrial jury'.

THE ORGANISATION OF EMPLOYMENT TRIBUNALS

The President of the Employment Tribunals (a judicial officer appointed by the Lord Chancellor) is responsible for their running, assisted by a

Central Office of Employment Tribunals (COET) in London (there is also one in Glasgow for Scotland, with a President of Employment Tribunals for Scotland) which keeps a public register of all ET applications and decisions. The system is divided into regions, with a number of Regional Offices of Employment Tribunals (ROETs), each with a regional chairman, and ETs sit at these regional centres and at a number of permanent centres. Applications are lodged at the appropriate local ET.

The Employment Tribunal Service (ETS), which is part of the DTI, has responsibility for the overall administration of ETs. It has a director appointed by and who reports to the Secretary of State for Trade and Industry.

PROCEDURE

Only an outline of the procedure of the ETs can be given here. Essentially, ETs have an overriding objective which is 'to deal with cases justly'. This means dealing with cases, 'so far as practicable', so as to ensure that the parties are on an equal footing, saving expense (legal aid is not available in ETs), dealing with cases in ways proportionate to their complexity, and ensuring that they are dealt with expeditiously and fairly. There is no requirement to use any special form to commence proceedings in the ET, although there is a standard form (an ET1) which may be lodged as the originating application within the relevant time limit. In unfair dismissal and discrimination cases, for example, this is three months, whereas it is six months in redundancy payments claims and equal pay claims. The ET has discretion to extend this limit.

Employment Tribunals have the power to strike out a 'misconceived' claim (or defence – known as the Notice of Appearance). This is defined as one with 'no reasonable prospect of success'. The idea is that hopeless claims are not allowed to proceed to the hearing. Similarly, it may strike out 'scandalous ... or vexatious' claims. A copy of the claim is sent to the respondent employer, together with form ET3 on which the respondent may set out its response, which must be made within twenty-one days, although the ET may extend this limit where it was not reasonably practicable to respond in the time stipulated. A copy of the ET1 is also sent to ACAS, with a view to possible settlement before the hearing with the assistance of an ACAS conciliation officer.

Employment tribunals may make orders for the discovery (or disclosure as it is now called under the Civil Procedure Rules (CPR)) and/or inspection of documents, further particulars of the claim or the Notice of Appearance, or to provide written answers to any question. They may also order a pre-hearing review (PHR), either on the application of one of the parties, or on their own motion, where it appears that an aspect of the claim or defence is unlikely to succeed. Pre-hearing reviews may be heard by a chairperson sitting alone. Where the ET decides that the aspect of the claim in question is unlikely to succeed, it can impose a condition that a party pays a deposit of up to £500 within twenty-one days before being allowed to continue with the proceedings. Further, the party upon whom such a condition is imposed is warned that an order for costs could be made against them at the full hearing, together with forfeiture of the deposit.

THE HEARING

Although ETs are allowed to regulate their own procedure, their proceedings tend to be quite formal, akin to civil court proceedings. If possible, the parties should agree in advance of the hearing the documents to be used before the ET, usually contained within a Bundle of Documents, for ease of reference. The party with the burden of proof starts, e.g. in an unfair dismissal case where the employer accepts that dismissal has taken place this will be the employer. However, in a constructive unfair dismissal case, where the fact of dismissal is in dispute, it is the employee who starts. Witnesses give evidence on oath and undergo examination-in-chief and cross-examination. When all witnesses have given their evidence, closing submissions are made by each side, and the ET retires to consider its decision.

The ET may reserve its decision until a later date or give its decision orally at the conclusion of the hearing, with the written decision setting out summary reasons being sent out some time later. However, the parties may request full written reasons either at the hearing or within twenty-one days of dispatch of the summary reasons. In discrimination and equal pay cases, full written reasons are provided.

COSTS

Although costs are not normally awarded by the ET, it does have power to make a costs order against a party (or a party's representative) where, in bringing the proceedings, the party or the representative has 'acted vexatiously, abusively, disruptively or otherwise unreasonably, or the bringing or conducting of the proceedings by a party has been misconceived', up to a maximum of £10,000.

Employment Tribunals may review their decisions, either of their own motion or upon the application of a party, within fourteen days of promulgation. There are very limited grounds for review, e.g. a clerical error, or that the decision was made in the absence of one party. An appeal may be made to the Employment Appeal Tribunal on a point of law within six seeks of the promulgation of the decision.

EMPLOYMENT APPEALS

The Employment Appeal Tribunal (EAT) was established in 1975 under the Employment Protection Act 1975 (EPA), although it is now regulated by the ETA and regulations made thereunder. It hears appeals from the ETs on points of law (not fact). A president is appointed for a term of three years from the ranks of High Court judges. Its composition is similar to that of ETs, in that it has two lay members drawn from employers' and employees' organisations (although these tend to be fairly senior members with wide experience, compared with lay members of the ET), but the chairperson is a High Court judge or circuit judge. Part-time recorders who also appear as counsel in the EAT are not allowed to sit as chairpersons of the EAT following the House of Lords in *Lawal* v. *Northern Spirit Ltd* (2003) that this practice tended to undermine public confidence in the judicial system. As in the ET, the judge may be outvoted by the lay members. A judge sitting alone in the EAT may hear appeals from a single-member ET, and the EAT may consist of the chairperson and one lay member where the parties agree to this. Unlike the ET, legal aid is available in the EAT. As appeals are made to the EAT on points of law, it is much more usual for the parties to have legal representation in this forum. Although proceedings are not quite as formal or legalistic as in the High Court, they are more formal than in the ETs.

The EAT is a court of record and, as such, its decisions must be followed by ETs and inferior courts. However, different divisions of the EAT are not obliged to follow their own decisions, which can lead to confusion at ET level about what is the correct legal analysis to be applied. The English EAT sits in London (the Scottish EAT sits in

Edinburgh). Appeals from the EAT are to the Court of Appeal and then to the House of Lords.

Court of Appeal and House of Lords

Once a case is appealed from the EAT to the Court of Appeal and beyond, it leaves the specialist tribunals set up to deal with labour law matters and moves into the ordinary civil court system. Clearly, cases reaching these higher courts are of wider public interest and, in appeals to the House of Lords, they must concern a matter of public importance.

European Court of Justice

The European Court of Justice (ECJ) has been immensely significant in the development of labour law within the United Kingdom, particularly in the field of sex discrimination and equal pay. Any court or tribunal, including ETs, from within the jurisdiction may refer a case to the ECJ under Article 234 for a ruling on the correct interpretation of EU law, or on its applicability within the domestic legal system. It should be noted that the ECJ's rulings on, for example, whether directives have been correctly implemented by the Member States, or whether English labour law complies with our obligations under EU law, has been immensely significant in the field of labour law. The ECJ does not decide the issue before the domestic court or tribunal, it simply provides a ruling on the questions put to it by the domestic court, and it is for that court to decide the matter in the light of the ruling given by the ECJ.

TIME LIMITS

When Employment Tribunals were originally set up, the idea was that they would provide cheap, informal and quick legal remedies. For this reason, time limits in tribunals are shorter than in some other courts. Generally speaking, claims must be brought within three months of either the date of an employee's dismissal or the act complained of, although there are some exceptions.

The person bringing the claim is now known as the 'claimant'. Examples of where the time limit is different are shown in Table 11.1. The

Table 11.1   Examples of different time limits for bringing a claim to the ET

Claim	Time limit
Unfair dismissal for official industrial action	6 months from date of dismissal
Redundancy payment	6 months starting with the relevant date
Equal pay	6 months from the date employment ceased
Interim relief pending complaint of unfair dismissal	7 days immediately following termination
Contract counter-claim by employer	6 weeks from receipt of details of an employee's contractual claim

party against whom the claim is made (the 'respondent') must then file a response within a prescribed time scale. As from 1 October 2004 the prescribed time scale is twenty-eight days. It should be noted that, with regard to the submission of both claims and defences, whilst it is possible to apply for an extension of time, failure to observe the time limits commonly results in a claim or defence being refused by the tribunal.

The tribunal on the day has wide discretion to determine how the hearing is conducted, including the order in which the parties present their case, i.e. in which the witnesses are called. Nevertheless it is fairly standard for the order to be as follows, depending upon the type of claim. (The following list includes only the main types of tribunal claim.) When talking about who goes first and second, this covers all the evidence to be given on behalf of that party. Only in very rare circumstances (e.g. where a witness has flown in especially for the case) will the tribunal agree to interpose a witness on behalf of the claimant whilst the respondent is giving evidence, and vice versa.

In other words if, as with unfair dismissal cases (excluding constructive dismissal), the respondent has gone first, then all the respondent's witnesses will give their evidence and be cross-examined before it is the turn of the claimant and the claimant's witnesses.

REMEDIES

At the end of proceedings, the tribunal must give its decision on the merits of the case (other than in rare circumstances where it might instead remit the case for a rehearing by another tribunal) and its reasons for that decision.

The judgment and reasons may be communicated to the parties in one of three ways:

1 The chairman may announce both the judgment and reasons together, by dictating into a recording machine in the presence of the parties, after the end of the hearing.
2 The chairman may announce the judgement only, reserving the reasons to be set out in writing at a later date.
3 The tribunal may reserve both its judgment and its reasons for promulgation at a later date.

REFORMS – SINCE OCTOBER 2004

Since October 2004, these new regulations came into force the tribunal or a chairman can issue a judgment which is the final determination of the proceedings or a particular issue, and orders which are issued in relation to interim matters and require a person to do or not to do something.

Judgments are issued at the end of a hearing and may be issued orally or be reserved to be given in writing at a later date.

If the judgment is given orally then reasons must be given at that time. Unless there is a request at the hearing or within a period of fourteen days from the date, the judgment is sent to the parties; no written reasons will be provided save if asked for by the Employment Appeal Tribunal.

If the judgment is reserved and sent to the parties later it must also contain the reasons for the judgment. Rule 30(6) sets out the information that must be included in written reasons for a judgment:

1 The issues which were identified as being relevant to the claim.
2 If issues were not determined, what those issues were and why they were not determined.
3 Findings of fact relevant to the issues which have been determined.
4 A concise statement of the applicable law.
5 How the relevant findings of fact and applicable law have been applied in order to determine the issues.
6 Where the judgment includes an award of compensation or a determination that one party should make a payment to the other, a table showing how the amount or sum has been calculated or a description of the manner in which it has been calculated.

Whenever a tribunal awards compensation or reaches a determination whereby a party is required to pay a sum of money to another (excluding an award of costs or allowances), the decision must contain a statement of the amount of compensation awarded or of the sum to be paid. Such a statement must be followed by a table or description explaining how it has been calculated. This rule applies to all decisions, regardless of whether they are in summary or extended form.

The tribunal clerk will then send the judgment and reasons to the Secretary of the Tribunals, who enters the document in the register at the Central Office of Employment Tribunals and sends a copy to each of the parties and to any other person who made an appearance in the case.

ACAS

The Advisory Conciliation and Arbitration Service (ACAS), as noted in Chapter 1, is a government-funded body involved in conciliation and has a statutory role to encourage the settlement of tribunal claims. As soon as a tribunal claim is made, ACAS is informed and an ACAS officer is sent copies of all correspondence between the parties and the tribunal. The parties can use the ACAS officer as a useful intermediary for the purposes of any settlement negotiation, in the confidence that any discussions through ACAS cannot be reported to the tribunal and that they will remain confidential.

The duty of the ACAS officer to promote settlement is also useful because the ACAS officer has powers to document settlements without needing lawyers, through the use of a special settlement agreement called a 'COT3' (and it's free!). The ACAS officer will help in negotiating the terms of the COT3, finalise the COT3, and withdraw the claim on the party's behalf once settlement has been reached.

INTERACTIVE LEARNING

1   Explain the procedure before an Employment Tribunal, listing the key features and consequences of non-compliance.
2   Devise a litigation strategy for handling employment law complaints at work.

12

Employment Relations

Businesses are effective when people management works! When it fails, employment relations become centre-stage. To that end, although this text has predominantly covered individual employment law, this chapter briefly examines the vast area of collective labour law (see Chapter 1 for detailed definitions). This chapter considers the law relating to trade unions, union recognition, collective bargaining, consultation and industrial action.

TRADE UNIONS

Trade unions, or the combination of workers, remained illegal associations because they restricted the terms on which each member would sell his labour (*Hornby* v. *Close* (1867)) until 1900. Today a trade union is defined in s. 1 of the Trade Union and Labour Relations (Consolidation) Act 1992 (hereinafter referred to as TULRCA 1992) as 'an organisation (whether temporary or permanent) … which consists wholly or mainly of workers of one or more descriptions and whose principal purposes include the regulation of relations between workers of that description or those descriptions and employers or employers' associations'.

Similarly, an employers' association is defined by TULRCA 1992, s. 122, as organisations (whether or not they are temporary or permanent) consisting wholly or mainly of employers or individual owners of undertakings and having among their principal purposes the regulation of relations between those employers and workers or trade unions. Unlike a trade union, an employers' association can be either an incorporated or unincorporated body. Where an association is unincorporated, it has the same rights and obligations as a trade union.

In legal terms, trade unions are unincorporated associations (i.e. they are not corporate bodies with a separate legal 'personality'), but they are given quasi-corporate status by TULRCA 1992, s. 10. The effect of this is that unions are able to make contracts, sue and be sued in relation to contract, tort or other matters, hold property via trustees, and have criminal proceedings taken against them, but for all other purposes they are treated as unincorporated associations.

In order to legally exist a trade union must attain a certificate of independence. This is applied for at the Certification Office. The test of independence in TULRCA 1992, s. 5, is in two parts: it requires that a union 'is not under the domination or control of an employer'. Such was considered in *Blue Circle Staff Association* v. *Certification Officer* (1977). Consequently, the Certification Officer must consider in respect of each application by a trade union the following:

1   the history of the trade union/organisation;
2   its membership base;
3   its organisation and structure;
4   its finances;
5   employer-provided facilities;
6   its negotiating record.

The Certification Officer certifies and makes periodic checks that a union is maintaining its independence, since he may withdraw certificates if the characterisation of the union changes. An appeal from the Certification Officer to the EAT takes the form of a full re-hearing and 'the parties are not limited to the material presented to or considered by the Certification Officer in the course of his enquiries'.

A list of trade unions is maintained by the Certification Officer, an independent office established in 1975, and now enjoying wide-ranging administrative and judicial functions in relation to trade unions under the Employment Relations Act 2004.

By s. 46 of TULRCA 1992 every member of the principal executive committee of a trade union has to be elected every five years by all members of the union. Unions are subject to strict rules in relation to elections, as follows:

1 Balloting must be held in secret and preferably by postal voting.
2 There should be non-interference by 'the union or any of its members, officials or employees'.
3 Unions should finance all elections.

As an alternative to a postal vote, a union used to be able to conduct a semi-postal ballot or workplace ballot if the union was satisfied that there were no reasonable grounds to believe that this would not result in a free election as required by ss. 2 and 3 of the Trade Union Act 1984.

TRADE UNION RIGHTS

The exact scope of the activities of trade unions is open to interpretation. The ACAS Code of Practice on Time Off for Trade Union Duties confirms this statement.

However, case law has further expanded this rather narrow approach to include:

1 seeking union recognition;
2 discussing union matters (*Zucker* v. *Astrid Jewels Ltd* (1978));
3 seeking advice from union officials (*Stokes* v. *Wheeler-Green Ltd* (1979));
4 seeking to recruit new members (*Bass Taverns Ltd* v. *Burgess* (1995)).

Reasonable time should be given to such activities, including the holding of a meeting during the employers' time (see *Marley Tile Co. Ltd* v. *Shaw* (1980), *per* Goff LJ). The appropriate time for trade union activities is defined as not only occasions 'outside the employee's working hours' but also time 'within working hours at which, in accordance with arrangements agreed with, or consent given by his employer, it is permissible for him to take part in those activities' (TULRCA 1992, ss. 146(2), 170(2)). In *Post Office* v. *Union of Post Office Workers* (1974) Lord Reid declared that 'it does not include periods when in accordance with his contract the worker is on his employer's premises, but not actually working'. The time taken off must be reasonable as to amount and the circumstances when it is taken. For example, in *Wignall* v. *British Gas Corporation* (1984) the applicant had already been granted twelve weeks' leave for union business when he sought a further ten days for the preparation of a union district monthly magazine. The EAT upheld the tribunal's decision that it was reasonable for the employers to refuse the further time.

The ACAS Code of Practice on Time Off gives some indication of the duties for which time off should be granted:

1 collective bargaining with the appropriate level of management;
2 informing constituents about negotiations or consultations with management;
3 meetings with other lay officials or with full-time officials;
4 interviews with and on behalf of constituents on grievance and disciplinary matters;
5 appearing on behalf of constituents before an outside body.

COLLECTIVE AGREEMENTS

The statutory definition of a collective agreement can be found in TULRCA 1992 s. 178. It defines a collective agreement as 'any agreement or arrangement made by or on behalf of one or more trade unions and one or more employers or employers' associations' and relating to one or more of the following matters:

1 machinery for negotiation or consultation relating to the above, including recognition;
2 terms and conditions of employment;
3 engagement or non-engagement, or termination or suspension of employment or the duties of employment, of one or more workers;
4 matters of discipline;
5 a worker's membership or non-membership of a trade union;
6 facilities for trade union officials;
7 pay, including pensions, has been emphasised and added to the list.

TRADE UNION RECOGNITION

In effect, recognition is defined in TULRCA (1992) s. 178 as meaning 'recognition of the union by an employer, or two or more associated employers, to any extent, for the purpose of collective bargaining ...'.

Historically in the United Kingdom, union recognition has not been a compulsory process, but voluntary. The Employment Relations Act (EReLA) 1999 changed that and formally introduced a controversial new statutory recognition procedure, under which a union may claim recognition against the employer's wishes.

Under common law, recognition is an entirely voluntary process. In such circumstances, recognition occurs by agreement, as a matter of custom and practice and/or good employment relations, rather than through law. The established principles governing voluntary recognition are that pre-existing collective bargaining occurred expressly or impliedly, albeit evidenced (see *National Union of Tailors & Garment Workers* v. *Charles Ingram & Co. Ltd* (1977)).

The Employment Relations Act 1999 (as amended 2004) enacted a new statutory recognition procedure, whereby an employer has a legal duty to recognise an independent trade union (or trade unions) where a majority of the relevant work force seek it. The Employment Relations Act 1999 came into force on 6 June 2000, as amended 2004.

Under this statutory procedure, a new process applies where an independent trade union may apply to an employer for recognition in relation to a particular group of workers (a 'bargaining unit'). If the employer does not agree to recognise the union, or disputes the appropriate bargaining unit for the purposes of recognition, the union may apply to the Central Arbitration Committee to decide the appropriate bargaining unit and/or whether the union should be recognised. Subject to the circumstances, recognition can be automatic, or a ballot may need to be held. Where it is shown that a majority of the workers in the bargaining unit are members of the union, the CAC can declare the union recognised without a ballot; otherwise, a secret ballot of all the workers in the bargaining unit must be held. The recognition procedures do not apply where the employer employs fewer than twenty-one workers.

The statutory recognition procedure begins with a formal request for recognition to an employer. Two or more unions can apply jointly, but in such a case it must be shown that the unions will co-operate effectively in collective bargaining and, if the employer wishes, conduct single-table bargaining. The request must be in writing, must specify the union or unions and the bargaining unit in respect of which recognition is claimed, and must state that the request is made under Schedule A1, TULRCA 1992. The request will not be valid unless the union (or each of the unions) has a certificate of independence, and the employer (together with any associated employers) employs at least twenty-one workers on the day of the request, or an average of at least twenty-one workers in the thirteen weeks leading up to that day.

Where an application is made to the CAC, the CAC has ten days to decide whether the application is valid and admissible. The CAC cannot consider an application unless, in addition to the requirements already noted, it is satisfied that at least 10 per cent of the proposed bargaining unit are members of the union, and that a majority of workers in the proposed bargaining unit would be likely to favour recognition. If the CAC has been asked to decide on the appropriate bargaining unit, it must initially give the parties a further twenty-eight days to agree the bargaining unit. If the parties are still deadlocked, the CAC must determine the appropriate bargaining unit within ten days, taking into account the need for the bargaining unit to be compatible with effective management, and, so far as is consistent with that need, the following factors:

1   the views of the employer and the union (or unions);
2   existing national and local bargaining arrangements;
3   the desirability of avoiding small fragmented bargaining units within an undertaking;
4   the characteristics of the workers falling within the bargaining unit and of any other employees of the employer whom the CAC considers relevant;
5   the location of the workers.

The main rights accruing to an independent, recognised trade union in relation to consultation and the provision of information are:

1   to receive relevant information for the purposes of collective bargaining;
2   to be consulted in respect of collective (i.e. large-scale) redundancies;
3   to be consulted in relation to the transfer of an undertaking.

The CAC is headed by a chairperson (currently Burton J) and consists of a chairman, assisted by lay panel members, representing both employers and employees (see www.cac.gov.uk).

CONSULTATION AT WORK

The National Consultation and Information (NIC) Directive 2001 is based upon the social partnership approach. That is, workers should have the basic right to consultation, but a mechanism for bargaining should be agreed between the parties and utilised accordingly. This new law requires companies with fifty or more employees to regularly inform on the enterprises' economic situation and to consult workers on key decisions regarding the organisation's future. These include situations where jobs are threatened and where any anticipatory measures, such as training, skill development and other measures increasing the adaptability of employees, are planned. Consultation is also compulsory on decisions that are likely to lead to substantial changes in work organisation or in contractual relations. National governments will enact their own implementing measures, with sanctions for breaches, and are free to extend further these minimal information and consultation rights. From 2005 this law applies to organisations with 150 or more workers, from 2007 to businesses with over 100 workers and from 2008 to those with more than fifty workers.

INDUSTRIAL ACTION

'Industrial action' is defined as a strike or withdrawal of labour. The Employment Relations Act 2004 amended the law relating to industrial action, including measures to simplify the law relating to ballots for industrial action and ballot notices. Moreover, it strengthened the protection against the dismissal of workers taking official and lawful industrial action. The latter reform involves the exempting of employer 'lock-outs' for an eight-week period.

A 'strike' is defined in s. 246 of TULRCA 1992 as 'any concerted stoppage of work'. In *Connex South Eastern Ltd* v. *Rail Maritime and Transport Workers* (1999), the Court of Appeal held that the definition of 'strike' is broad enough to cover any refusal to work for periods when the workers would normally work. In most, if not all, strike action, contracts of employment are affected. However, no notice to terminate the contract is given. Even though strike action amounts to repudiation of contract.

Action, short of dismissing strikers, is that the employer is clearly not obliged to pay the striking workers during the industrial action itself. The general principle is that deductions from pay are regulated by agreement between the parties and by a statutory exception under s. 14(5) of ERA 1996.

Strike action is not the only form of industrial action. Other forms include work-to-rule and go-slow, as well as overtime bans. In addition, employees may work normally but refuse to perform the particular duty about which they are protesting. Sit-ins are another form of industrial action.

An employer may also resort to industrial action, since employers hold the right to make changes in their business. Consequently, employers may have cause to 'lock out' their work force.

Industrial action is lawful where:

1   the employers have a cause of action at common law; and or
2   those taking industrial action are acting in 'contemplation or furtherance of a trade dispute against the employer'. If so, s. 219 of TULRCA 1992 gives immunity from action which:

    (a)   induces a person to breach a contract of employment;
    (b)   threatens that a contract of employment will be breached;
    (c)   interferes with the trade, business or employment of a person;
    (d)   constitutes an agreement by two or more persons to procure the doing of any such act.

Consequently, when these torts emerged protection to trade unions was given, so as to grant them immunity from legal action. It is the so-called 'golden formula' that provides the protection. To be protected, the individual striker must be acting 'in contemplation or furtherance of a trade dispute' (TULRCA 1992 s. 219(2)).

However, the statutory immunities under s. 219 will be removed in the following situations:

1   secondary action;
2   unlawful picketing;
3   action to enforce union membership;
4   action to impose union recognition;
5   action in support of dismissed unofficial strikers;
6   action without proper notice to an employer;
7   action without a valid strike ballot.

INTERACTIVE LEARNING

1 Consider what unions must do to ensure that any industrial action taken is lawful.

2 Business UK plc is a consultancy firm. There is currently a dispute with its workers, whose union, No Go, has held a ballot and as a result taken industrial action over pay. Last week, a three-day strike took place and consequently Business UK plc lost money and a contract with Promote US Inc. Management at Business UK plc has found out that its workers were threatened not to attend work. Advise Business UK plc.

3 Devise a strategy for managing consultation where unions are and are not recognised.

Further Reading

Adnett, Nick and Hardy, Stephen (2005) *European Social Model*. Aldershot: Elgar Publications.

Chartered Institute of Personnel and Development (2003) *CIPD Employment Law for People Managers*. London: Chartered Institute of Personnel and Development.

Daniels, Kay (2003) *Employment Law for HR and Business Students*. Wimbledon: Chartered Institute of Personnel and Development.

Duddington, John (2003) *Employment Law*. Bristol: Jordans.

Hardy, Stephen (2001) *Understanding TUPE*. Oxford: Chandos Publishing.

Leighton, Patricia and Proctor, Giles (2003) *Recruiting within the Law,* 3rd edn. London: Chartered Institute of Personnel and Development.

Nairns, J. (2004) *Employment Law for Business Students*. Harlow: Longman.

Painter, Richard W. and Holmes, Ann E. M. (2004) *Cases and Materials on Employment Law*, 5th edn. Oxford: Oxford University Press.

Pitt, Gwyneth (2004) *Employment Law*, 5th edn. London: Sweet & Maxwell.

Tolley's, (2004) *Employment Law Handbook,* 17th edn. Croydon: Tolley.

Upex, Robert, Benny, Richard and Hardy, Stephen (2004) *Labour Law – Core Text*. Oxford: Oxford University Press.

Upex, Robert (2006) *Termination of Employment*, 3rd edn. Bristol: Jordans.

Wadham, John, Mountfield, Helen and Edmundson, Anna (2003) *Blackstone's Guide to the Human Rights Act 1998,* 3rd edn. Oxford: Oxford University Press.

Willey, Brian (2004) *Employment Law in Context*. Harlow: FT Longman.

Useful Websites

Advisory, Conciliation and Arbitration Service (ACAS)	www.acas.org.uk
Commission for Racial Equality	www.cre.gov.uk
Department of Trade and Industry	www.dti.gov.uk
Disability Rights Commission	www.drc.org.uk
Employment Appeal Tribunal	www.employmentappeals.gov.uk
Equal Opportunities Commission	www.eoc.org.uk
Government Information Service	www.ukonline.gov.uk
Health and Safety Executive	www.hse.gov.uk
Stationery Office	www.tso.co.uk
Law Commission	www.lawcom.gov.uk
Trades Union Congress	www.tuc.org.uk
British employment law	www.emplaw.co.uk
UK legal documents and information	www.uklegal.com

Index